String Quilt Style

Easy techniques and inspiring designs from strips, scraps and stash

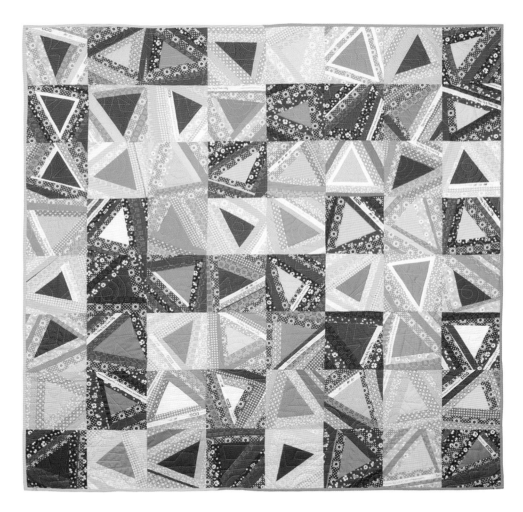

Mary M. Hogan

Landauer Publishing, LLC

String Quilt Style

Mary M. Hogan

Copyright © 2016 by Landauer Publishing, LLC
Projects Copyright © 2015
by Mary M. Hogan

This book was designed, produced,
and published by Landauer Publishing, LLC
3100 101st Street, Urbandale, IA 50322
515/287/2144   800/557/2144   landauerpub.com

President/Publisher: Jeramy Lanigan Landauer
Editor: Jeri Simon
Art Director: Laurel Albright
Designer, String Quilt Style: Lyne Neymeyer
Photographer: Sue Voegtlin

ISBN 13: 978-1-935726-82-1

Library of Congress: 2015952367

This book printed on acid-free paper.
Printed in United States

10-9-8-7-6-5-4-3-2-1

 FACEBOOK.COM/ LANDAUERPUBLISHING    YOUTUBE.COM/ LANDAUERPUBLISHING   PINTEREST.COM/ LANDAUERPUB

Contents

Start Stringing

String quilts are made by sewing fabric strips of all sizes to foundations. By using different fabrics and strings, each quilt is one-of-a-kind.

String quilting can be enjoyed by both beginning and experienced quilters. Since precision cutting and sewing are not crucial, beginning quilters can achieve immediate success. Those with more experience appreciate the break from exact piecing and sewing, and the chance to use leftover fabrics.

String quilts are the ultimate stash-busters. Fabric scraps, leftover blocks, fat quarters and unfinished projects can be cut into strings for a quilt. Since blocks can be made and put together in many ways the possibilities are endless.

String piecing techniques, design elements, and varying block placement are explained in separate sections. Each will be useful as you design and construct your own projects. The projects in the book highlight a number of the design elements and string piecing techniques.

Think Like a Designer

After you read this book my hope is that you will...
- Grab some fabric or UFOs
- Cut fabric strings
- Consider design elements, block types and layouts
- Make your own string quilt

About the Author

Mary Hogan, a self-taught sewer, began her sewing career making clothes for her dolls. In her teens, she moved into making garments, stuffed toys and dolls. After dabbling in numerous crafts, she found quilting in the 1990s. Now retired from her day job, Mary devotes more time to quilting, designing, and teaching.

She uses as many fabrics as possible in each quilt and likes improvisation, rarely knowing how a quilt will turn out when she begins. Mary has made countless quilts; she guesses it is well over 100, but less than 500. Like many quilters she has few quilts in her possession. Passionate about sharing quilting with others, she teaches regularly at The Quilting Season in Saline Michigan. She believes that classes should provide opportunities to learn, to practice new skills, and above all classes should be fun. This is Mary's first quilting book.

Mary has a BS in Nursing from Loyola University in Chicago, an MS in Public Health Nursing from the University of Illinois at Chicago, and a PhD from the University of Michigan and has held a variety of positions related to nursing and health care. She lives in Michigan with her husband, six sewing machines, and a growing stash of quilts, fabric, thread and yarn.

Tools and Foundations

Stitching string blocks is similar to stitching any pieced block, except the strings are sewn to a foundation. No specialty tools are required and only basic sewing supplies are needed.

ESSENTIAL TOOLS
- Rotary cutter and cutting mat
- Rulers
- Straight pins
- Flathead pins
- Sewing machine
- Thread
- Scissors

Mary's Favorite Tools
- 6" x 24" and 3" x 18" rulers
- 18" x 24" cutting mat for cutting strings
- Rotating cutting mat for trimming blocks
- Bent tweezers to remove bits of foundation
- Thread and 'leftover' bobbin threads
- AccuQuilt®Go! cutter and cutting dies to cut foundations and trim blocks

FOUNDATIONS

Foundations are not required for string blocks, but they make things easier. Foundations serve as patterns and keep blocks flat as strings are added. They also stabilize and support blocks as they are made.

Removable foundations include newsprint, copy paper, drawing paper, parchment paper, and coffee filters. Fabric strings are sewn to the paper foundations and trimmed. The paper is removed before sewing blocks together. These products can be found at office supply stores, restaurant suppliers and grocery stores.

Permanent foundations are left in place after blocks are trimmed. Muslin or other lightweight fabric has traditionally been used. Other options include lightweight interfacings and stabilizers. Permanent foundations provide extra strength, stability, weight or warmth in projects. These products can be purchased at craft and quilting stores.

CHOOSING A FOUNDATION

> ### Mary's Tips
> Questions to ask when choosing foundations
> Do I need...
> * Permanent or removable foundations?
>
> Are they...
> * Easy to cut?
> * Easy to remove?
> * Readily available?
> * Reasonable cost?

Removable foundations

* Newsprint (printed and unprinted)

  Newsprint is an excellent option for foundations and is readily available. The appeal of newsprint is it comes in relatively large sizes to fit any project and is easy to cut and remove. It may require ironing to flatten it before cutting.

  I do not recommend printed newspaper for white or very light fabrics. While I have not had a problem, it is possible that the newsprint could be transferred to your fabric.

  To alleviate any chance of print transfer, flat sheets and rolls of unprinted newsprint are available at craft and hobby stores. Packing paper also makes a great clean foundation.

* Parchment paper

  Parchment paper is available on a roll and the long strips can be used for border and column foundations. The paper provides excellent support, but may leave behind small bits of paper when removing the foundation.

* Coffee filters

  Coffee filters are the perfect foundation when making circle string blocks. They remove easily and provide good support. Coffee filters need to be pressed flat before being used as foundations.

* Brown paper lunch bags or Kraft paper on rolls

  Brown paper lunch bags and Kraft paper make excellent foundations. They are stiffer than other removable foundations so they provide excellent support when sewing. They are readily available, inexpensive and easy to remove. If using Kraft paper it should not be heavier than a 30 pound weight.

Other products to make removable foundations
* Magazine and phone book pages
* Printer and notebook paper
* Sketch rolls and pads
* Delicatessen papers
* Patty paper
* Candy and baking cups
* Pattern paper
* Sulky® Tear-Easy stabilizer
* Specialty papers (quilting paper, paper piecing paper, foundation paper, vellum)

Permanent foundations

A number of sewing-related products can be used as permanent foundations. Purchase small amounts of any product and test before planning the whole project. This will help determine if you like the feel of the finished piece and whether the product is easy to use.

* Muslin

  Muslin adds an extra layer of fabric to the project, providing additional weight and stability.

* Nylon tulle and net

  Nylon tulle is a material typically used in bridal veils, ballet outfits and dress clothes.

  Nylon tulle on a spool works well for making columns, sashings and borders, but it is not recommended for making blocks.

  Nylon net is similar to tulle, but has larger holes and feels coarser. It works well for making blocks and columns, but is more difficult to handle and cut than paper. It is lightweight and provides less support than many papers, but since the net remains in the blocks being lightweight is a bonus. If using net, cut the foundations larger than necessary.

  Net and tulle are not suitable to use as an accurate block pattern. Due to the open nature of both, it is also difficult to mark the foundations.

* Sheerweight Interfacing

  Interfacing is used to stiffen an area or to help maintain the shape of a finished garment. Many interfacings have fusible on one side. Use sheerweight interfacing; it is lighter than featherweight. When using interfacing, it is best to cut the foundations a little larger than the final block size. Some interfacings tend to 'draw up' as the strings are sewn to the foundation. Trim the blocks using a ruler instead of relying on the interfacing as the pattern.

- Lightweight embroidery stabilizers
There are a number of lightweight stabilizers for machine embroidery that can be used as permanent foundations. Because they are lightweight they do not add a lot of stiffness to the finished project. It is best to make the foundation a little larger than required and cut to the correct size when the block is complete. Because these products are often found on rolls and don't tear like paper, they are also a good choice for borders or columns.

- Batting
Batting can be used as a foundation for smaller items, such as bags, place mats, table runners or mug mats. When using batting as the foundation, cut it larger than the final size and use a walking foot when sewing strings to it.

CUTTING FOUNDATIONS

Foundations are usually cut to the unfinished block size. For example, you would need to cut an 8-½" foundation for an 8" finished block.

Stack 5-8 foundation papers and secure with flathead pins. Using a rotary cutter, mat and ruler, cut the foundations to the needed size.

If oversizing the foundations, cut them approximately 1" larger than the desired finished block size. Trim to the correct size after sewing the strings.

Mary's Favorite Cutters

I love to use my AccuQuilt®GO! Fabric Cutter and my GO! BIG AccuQuilt® Fabric Cutter for cutting foundations. It quickly cuts stacks of foundations accurately. I use a rotary cutter and mat to cut my foundations when there is not a cutting die the size I need.

I also use AccuQuilt® cutters for trimming up blocks. It is very accurate and I don't have to cut each of the four sides.

Mary's Favorite Foundations

Type of Foundation

Type of Foundation	
Removable foundations for diagonal square blocks	• Flat deli paper • Unprinted newsprint-type paper • Brown paper lunch bags
Removable foundations for string columns or borders	• Drawing paper on a roll • Parchment paper on a roll
Permanent foundations for stability but light in weight	• Inspira® Whisper Web Mesh Light • Sheerweight interfacing (fusible or non)
Permanent foundations for columns or borders	• Tulle on a spool • Inspira® Whisper Web Mesh Light
Permanent foundations for weight and warmth	• Muslin • Batting

Design Elements for String Quilts

Design elements are the things you think about and notice when making or looking at quilts. The basic design elements are the tools quilters use to achieve interesting and beautiful quilts.

COLOR

Most quilters will tell you that color and fabric drew them to quilting. Color is also the first thing most people notice when looking at a quilt. There are three components to color.

Hue - the shade or name of the color—blue, green, gray, purple, etc.

Intensity - the strength or vividness of a color

Value - the lightness or darkness of a color; the lightest color value is white and the darkest is black

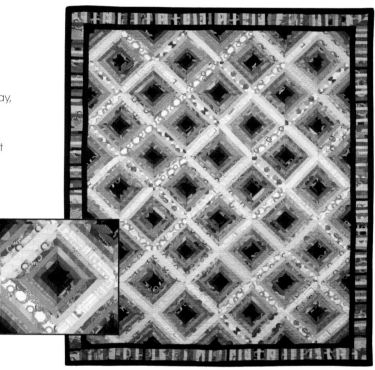

It is predominantly value and the contrast between values that create the images we see. Hue may be secondary. In the Juggling Summer quilt, on-point squares are formed by the light fabrics and dark centers of each square. Bits of red and orange are noticeable, but secondary to the shapes created by the value differences.

FOCAL POINT

The focal point is the center of interest; where the viewer's eye is drawn. When looking at a quilt, viewer's see the big picture and focal point before focusing on the details.

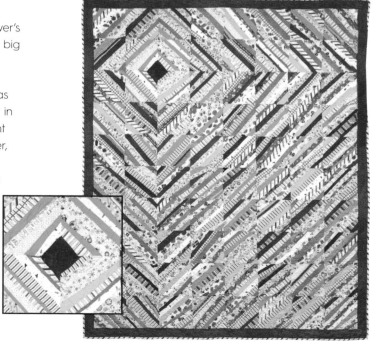

The It's a Jolly Holiday quilt uses a wonky red square as the focal point. Red is also used as a unifying element in several ways. The red lines echo around the focal point throughout the quilt. It is introduced again in the border, which helps draw out the focal point and echoing red lines. Note that the focal point, the center of interest, is not in the center of the quilt. Keep in mind that not every quilt needs a focal point.

PROPORTION

Proportion is the balance of the size of the parts in relation to the whole and to the other parts of the quilt. Proportion is considered when deciding string width, block size and the width of sashing and borders. For string blocks, proportion is particularly important when choosing the size of strings in relation to block size. Using wide strings on small blocks may not be as pleasing as using narrow strings.

UNITY AND VARIETY

A unified quilt is accomplished by using similar shapes, colors or fabric styles, so the resulting project looks like it belongs together. Variation is added when the lines, shapes and colors are not too similar; variation keeps the quilt interesting and adds surprise.

My Blue Heaven quilt uses a green graphic print as the center string of each block. Blue prints, solids and some selvages make up the rest of the blocks. There is one reverse color block.

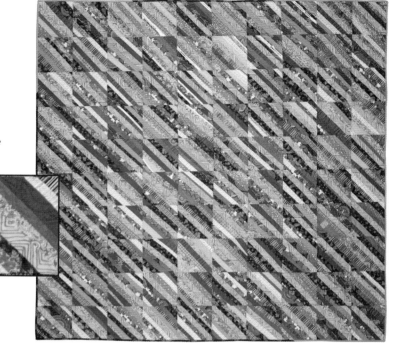

Blue is the unifying element in the quilt, but the green adds variety and a bit of fun. The blocks are all oriented in one direction with the green strings creating lines. Differing string widths, fabric styles and values create additional variety.

LINE AND SHAPE

Lines and shapes such as squares, triangles, and circles are created by blocks, strings within blocks, combining blocks and sashing between blocks.

Quilters notice the shapes created by block designs and layouts. The lines created by sashing within and between blocks are also part of the design.

The use of dark and light values in Uncle Ernie's Rocker quilt creates a striking set of squares set on point. The red center string in each block connects visually with the same string in other blocks, as shown in the quilt center.

FABRIC STYLE

There are many categories of fabric, including Civil War era reproductions, novelty prints, solids, batiks, 1930's reproductions, geometric, floral and many more

Fabric style can unify a quilt design. For example, Uncle Ernie's Rocker quilt on page 64 uses only Civil War reproduction fabrics, which gives the quilt a traditional look. Batik fabrics are used in the String Circles quilt on page 118. In the Summertime Coverlet on page 78 uses 1930's-style fabrics and solids.

Combining different fabric styles adds variation to quilts. The Leftover Columns quilt on page 122 combines many fabric styles to create an interesting quilt. Fabric styles include Civil War reproductions, large floral prints, solids, batiks and abstract and representational prints. By not limiting the quilt to one style, it became a great stash-buster.

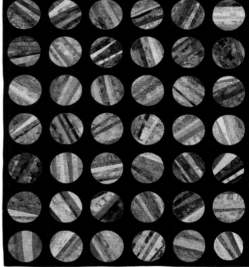

FABRIC LINE

Fabric lines are collections of coordinated fabrics from a specific designer or fabric company. Fabric lines change frequently. They are coordinated and meant to be used together, making it easier for the quilter who does not feel confident in choosing colors. When there is not enough variation in a fabric line, consider adding other fabrics.

The Fan quilt was created with a collection of fat quarters from Modern Mixers by Studio*e* Fabrics®. Coordinating solids were used for the fan centers.

The Tumbling Triangles quilt is made from the Pie Making Day fabric line by Brenda Ratliff for RJR Fabrics. Additional solids were added to the quilt.

Mary's Musings

I love bright prints, solids and blenders, but went outside my comfort zone to work with other fabric styles. While worried about mixing lots of fabric styles in the Leftover Columns quilt, I was happy with the result. Sometimes it's good to take a chance.

String Block Designs

String blocks can produce a variety of designs depending on how the blocks are made and combined. Color, value, placement and width of strings influence design. When blocks are sewn together, new shapes and lines emerge. Several examples are shown on the following pages and have been incorporated into some of the projects in this book. As you gain confidence, you will begin designing your own unique string blocks.

DIAGONAL SQUARE BLOCK DESIGN
Diagonal squares are the basic building blocks for the majority of string-pieced quilts in this book. Strings are sewn diagonally to a foundation square and then trimmed.

 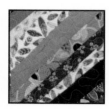 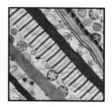

Orderly, Controlled Diagonal Block Designs
Many quilts love use repeating blocks and parallel lines in blocks, borders and sashing to create a sense of order. These designs tend to be predictable, soothing and satisfying. Placing strips in a methodical way produces a sense of order within the designs.

To achieve an orderly block design, try one of the following examples:

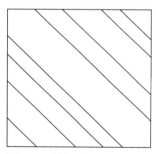

Diagonal block

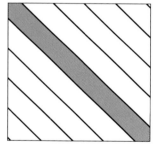

Use the same string size and color down the center of the block.

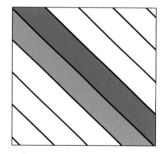

Place two strings in different colors at the center of the block.

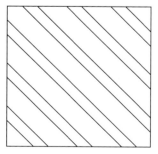

Alternate the size of the strings within the block.

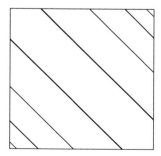

Begin with a large string in the block's center. Gradually make the strings smaller toward the block corners.

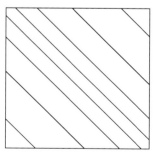

Begin with a small string in the block's center. Gradually make the strings wider toward the block corners.

Wonky, Irregular Diagonal Block Designs

There are many opportunities in string quilting to add variation. Wonky and irregular blocks have strings placed on the diagonal but these strings are not perfectly aligned. Crooked centers, variation in string width and disappearing strings all add interest to the blocks. Disappearing strings don't necessarily continue from one end of the foundation to the other. The majority of projects in this book have string size and placement variation

To achieve a wonky block design, try one of the following examples:

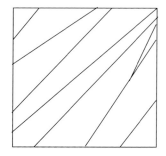

This very wonky example includes a variety of string widths, disappearing strings and a crooked center.

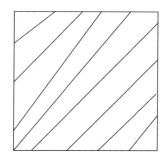

The example shown is somewhat wonky with a variety of string widths and a crooked center.

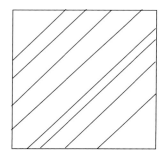

The slightly wonky example uses strings in a variety of widths.

Mary's Musings

I was heavily influenced by Gwen Marston's book *Liberated Quiltmaking* (Marston, 1996). It gave me permission to create non-traditional quilts and use irregularly shaped piecing. The fun and variety of this style pulled me right in.

Combining Diagonal Blocks

Diagonal blocks can be combined to create a variety of designs that suggest different shapes or lines. The following examples combine four or more blocks to achieve a desired design.

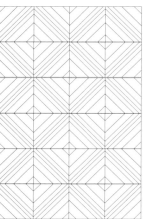

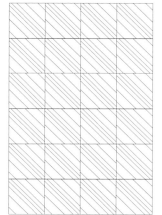
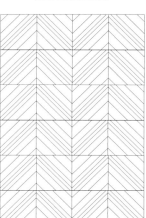

FAN BLOCK DESIGNS

Corner fan blocks are created when the strings converge in one corner.

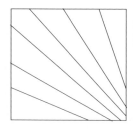  

Side fan blocks are created when the strings converge on one side.

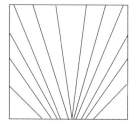

Combining Corner Fan Blocks

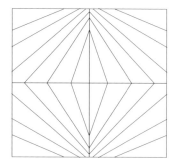 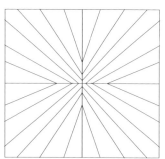 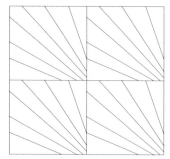 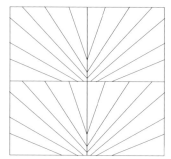

Combining Side Fan Blocks

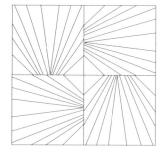 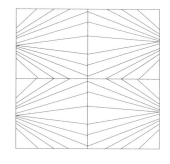 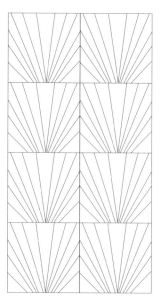

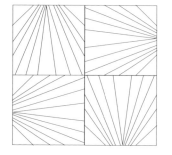 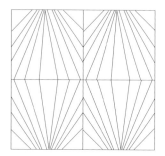

CIRCLE BLOCK DESIGN

Sewing strings to a circle foundation, such as a coffee filter, creates a string circle after trimming. The circles can then be appliquéd to fabric squares. The String Circles quilt was made this way.

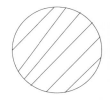  

Combining String Circles

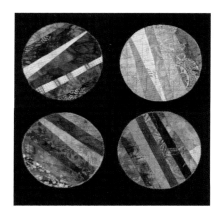  

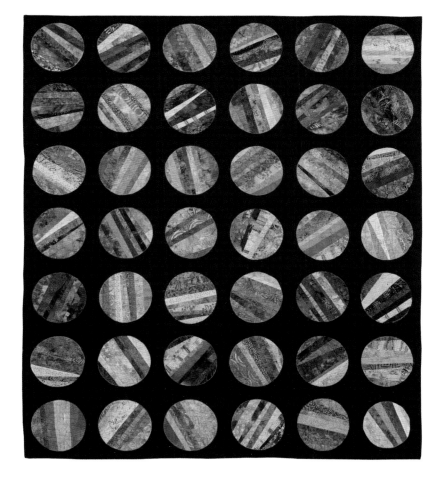

HALF-SQUARE TRIANGLE BLOCK DESIGNS

Cover half the foundation square with fabric strings. Stitch a solid or white fabric piece on the other half. The Selvage Pinwheels quilt on page 92 uses half-square triangle blocks.

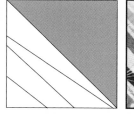  

Cover half the foundation square with fabric strips. The other half of the foundation will be trimmed to create a half-square string triangle. The Solid Squares quilt on page 112 uses half-square string triangles for the corner and side-setting triangles.

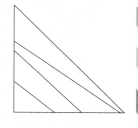 

Cover each half of the square with strings perpendicular to the other. Combine the blocks in groups of four to create different designs. See design examples below.

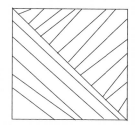 

Combining Half-Square Triangle Blocks

Half-square triangle blocks are versatile in creating additional designs. Flying geese, pinwheels and square-in-a-square are just a few of the designs made with these string blocks.

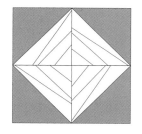 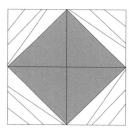 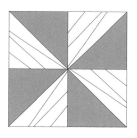 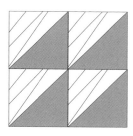 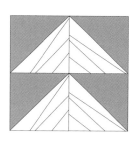

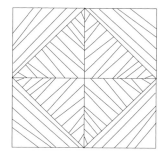 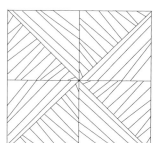 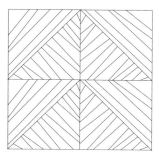

WONKY TRIANGLE BLOCK DESIGNS

Place fabric triangles in varying positions on foundation squares and surround them with strings to create these blocks.

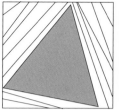  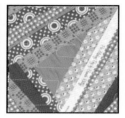

Combining Wonky Triangle Blocks

Achieve a variety of block designs by altering the size and position of the triangle. A variety of colorful wonky triangle blocks placed randomly will create a fun quilt design. The Tumbling Triangles quilt on page 108 uses wonky triangle blocks.

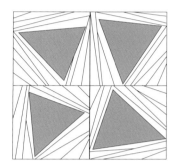 

ISOSCELES TRIANGLE BLOCK DESIGNS

Place a fabric isosceles triangle at the bottom of a foundation square. Cover the rest of the square with strings to complete the block.

Combining Isosceles Triangle Blocks

The isosceles triangle blocks are stacked or rotated to make diamonds and pinwheels.

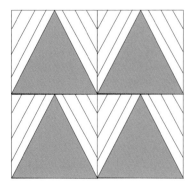 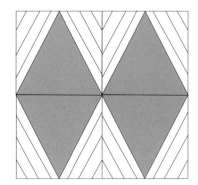 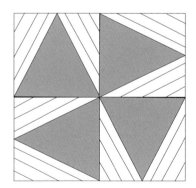

ONE-BLOCK DIAMOND DESIGN

For the one-block diamond design, choose a coordinating fabric as the foundation. Mark the diamond shape on the fabric and sew strings to the outer corners.

TWO-BLOCK DIAMOND DESIGN

The two-block diamond design uses two isosceles triangle blocks. Stitch the two blocks together to make the diamond.

FOUR-BLOCK DIAMOND DESIGN

Unlike the previous block designs, diamond blocks require a rectangular foundation. Light value strips are sewn to one side of the diagonal center and dark value strips are sewn to the other. The four-block diamond design is created with two pairs of mirror-image blocks or a total of four blocks. Refer to the diagrams for examples.

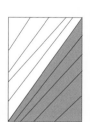

Light center
diamond design

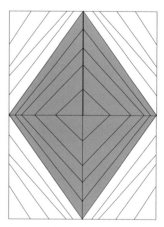

Dark center
diamond design

RECTANGULAR ROWS OR COLUMNS

Rectangular rows or columns can also be string pieced. Similar to diagonal block designs, the rows can be pieced with strings that are consistent or vary in size. Columns can be made so they are migrating to the left or right, or going straight across. The Leftover Columns quilt below is a quick project that uses string-pieced columns in different sizes with sashing.

Strings migrating to right

Strings migrating to left

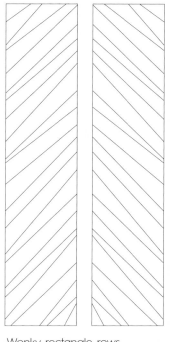

Wonky rectangle rows

Combining Rectangular Columns

Alternate the direction of string-pieced columns. You can also vary the width of columns.

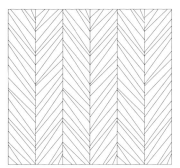

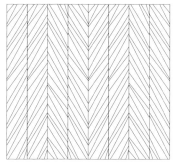

Block and Quilt Layouts

Add the design elements discussed on pages 8-11 to blocks. When blocks are combined in the quilt layout new shapes and lines are formed. Lines, shapes and unifying elements can be added to blocks through value and color placement. Designs can also be created through use of a particular fabric or contrasting value in the center or in the corners of blocks. The following examples show a variety of ways to incorporate basic design elements into block and quilt layouts.

Think Like a Designer

Use blocks to create a design in the quilt layout.

Highlight by using
- The same fabric or color
- Contrasting value

Places to highlight
- Center of blocks
- One or both corners
- Center and corners

Alter size of center or corners
Combine block types

QUILT LAYOUTS WITH DIAGONAL BLOCKS

One Dark Value String Running Diagonally Through the Center of the Block

A dark value center string creates a clear line within each block.

A square-in-a-square shape is created when four blocks are joined together.

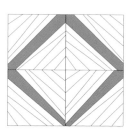

A secondary design of blocks set-on-point with sashing emerges when the blocks are placed in a quilt design.

The unifying element is seen due to the dark value center string. For a more orderly quilt top, use the same size strings and placement for the blocks.

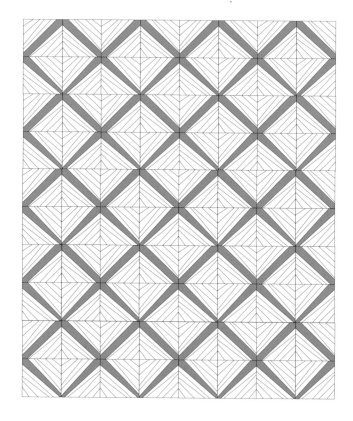

One Dark Value String Running Diagonally Through the Center of the Block

A colored center string in a consistent width creates a clear line within each block.

The blocks are oriented in the same direction when sewn together to create parallel diagonal lines.

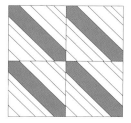

The consistently sized center string and the block layout create a unifying element in the quilt design.

A Single Color Used In Only One Corner of the Block

A single color used only in the corner of the block provides a unifying element.

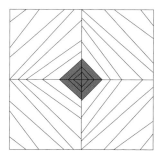

A center diagonal square is formed when four blocks are joined together.

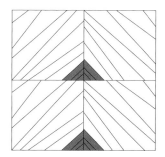

Form center triangles by stacking pairs of blocks together.

Same Color In Opposite Corners of the Block

Identical size strings of the same color are used in opposite corners of the block. The identical string size and color unify the blocks.

Center squares are formed when four blocks are joined together.

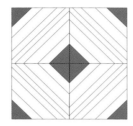

A secondary design that includes corner squares emerges when the blocks are placed in a quilt design. The center squares can also serve as the focal points in the quilt top.

Two Colors In Opposite Corners

For more visual impact, use larger strings in two colors in opposite corners of the block.

Large center squares are formed when four blocks are joined together. This also adds to the visual impact of the quilt.

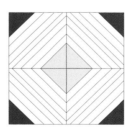

Use large and small strings in opposite corners of the block to create different size corner triangles and center squares.

Using the Same Color for Both Center String and Corners

The center string and block corners use the same fabric creating a distinct line.

When four blocks are joined together a new center shape appears.

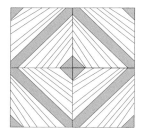
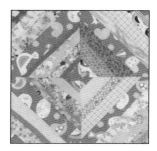

A secondary design of blocks set-on-point with sashing emerges when the blocks are placed in a quilt design.

The unifying element is seen in the center strings and block corners with the same fabric. For a more orderly quilt top, use the same size strings and placement for the blocks.

Using Identical Strings in the Same Diagonal Position

Place identical strings (same fabric and width) in the same diagonal position on four foundation squares.

When the four blocks are joined together the strings will match producing concentric sets of squares radiating from the center. This creates an orderly and interesting quilt design.

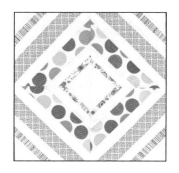

QUILT LAYOUTS WITH FAN BLOCKS

Using Combination of Blocks to Produce the Illusion of Diamonds

A dark value center string creates a clear line within each fan block.

Four fan blocks joined together create an 'X' shape.

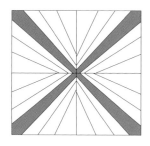

When the blocks are placed in the quilt design the 'X' pattern is clearly visible. A secondary diamond design emerges from the lighter value strings.

Using a Dark Center String to Create a Line

A dark value center string creates a line within the fan block.

Join four blocks in the same parallel orientation.

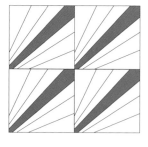

The parallel orientation of fan blocks creates directional unity in the quilt design.

Using a Single Color in Block Corner

A single color used in one block corner provides a unifying element. The diagonal strings create directional lines.

When four blocks are joined together a center diagonal square is formed. A radiating design also emerges.

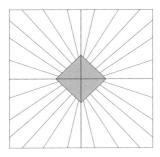

When the blocks are placed in the quilt design the radiating design is clearly visible. Two unifying elements are the color of the center diagonal squares and the consistent width of the diagonal strings.

Form center triangles by stacking pairs of blocks together.

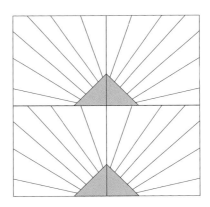

Finishing Elements
Sashing, Borders, Backs, Quilting and Binding

SASHING AND BORDERS

Sashing and borders are common components in quilt designs. Sashing separates blocks, or rows of blocks, to add a line element. Borders are used to frame the quilt design and give it a finished look. Borders are also an opportunity to add another element of design.

Proportion, particularly width, plays an important role in sashing and borders. You don't want these components to overwhelm the blocks or quilt design. However, if they are too narrow they may have little impact. Audition various widths for sashing and borders by laying blocks out on fabric.

SASHING WITHIN SETS OF FOUR BLOCKS

Sashing can be used within sets of four blocks. Sashing creates new lines and shapes.

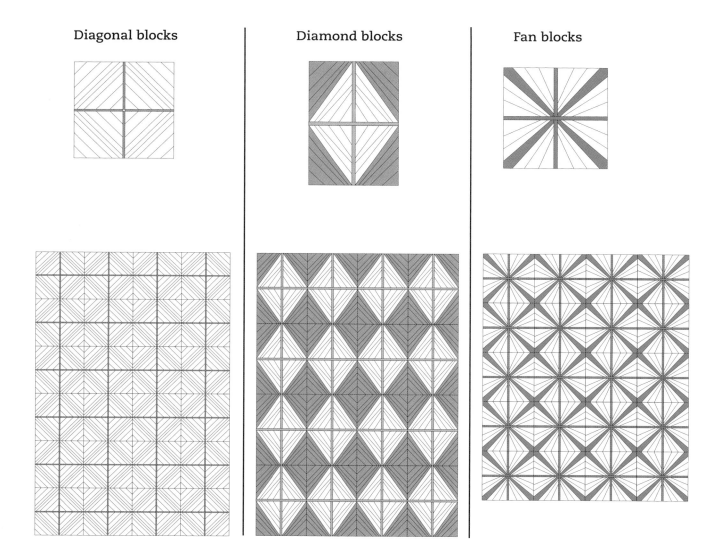

| Diagonal blocks | Diamond blocks | Fan blocks |

SASHING AROUND BLOCKS

Sashing can be used around sets of four blocks to set them apart. It can also be used for diagonal, fan or diamond blocks. In the quilt design, sashing would be used between the block rows and sets of blocks.

Diagonal blocks

Diamond blocks

Fan blocks

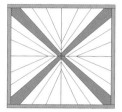

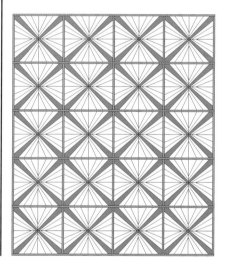

Think Like a Designer

Ask yourself these questions...
- Do I have unifying elements and variety?
- How big do I want my quilt?
- How hard do I want to work?
- Do I want this project to be organized and precise or random and wonky?

Adding sashing can help achieve a unified, organized quilt. If you want to make your quilt a bit larger, sashing can also accomplish that, but you may have to work a little harder.

SASHING WITHIN AND AROUND BLOCKS

Sashing within and around blocks can add additional lines and shapes, especially in a fan block layout. For a diagonal block layout it is often easier to let the center strings act as the sashing. In the quilt design, sashing would be used between the block rows and within and around sets of blocks.

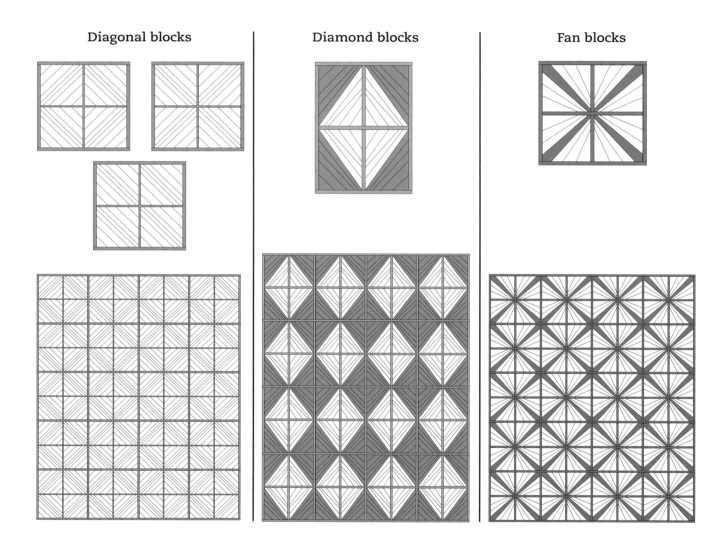

Diagonal blocks   **Diamond blocks**   **Fan blocks**

SASHING BETWEEN COLUMNS

Sashing between columns and rows adds straight lines, breaking up the angled columns. The sashing can be wide or narrow and placed between single columns or groups of columns.

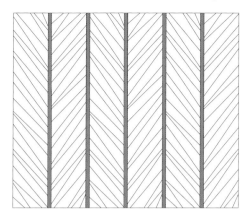  

BORDERS

Single Border

Borders using a single fabric are a good choice for quilts with a busy design. They give the eye a resting place without detracting from the quilt design. The It's A Jolly Holiday quilt on page 68 is an example of a single border.

String Border

A string border is a good way to frame a scrappy quilt. It is made with varying widths of the fabrics used in the quilt. The Juggling Summer quilt on page 102 has a string border.

Diagonal Column Border

A diagonal column border gives the quilt a feeling of movement. The UFO quilt on page 82 uses diagonal column borders and includes many fabrics used in the project.

String Zigzag Border

Small-scale diagonal blocks make an interesting border. Arrange the border blocks so they create a zigzag pattern. The Simple Modern Squares quilt on page 96 uses a zigzag border.

No Border

Borders are not always necessary for every quilt design. Modern quilters are less likely than traditional quilters to use borders. The String Circles quilt on page 118 does not have a border.

QUILT BACKS

The back of a quilt provides another occasion to design and play. When making string quilts you inevitably have strings leftover after the quilt top is complete. Include a column of strings, extra blocks or other leftover pieces to your quilt back.

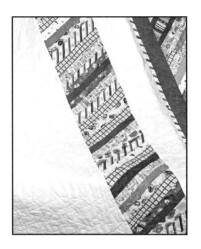

QUILTING

Elaborate quilting would be lost on scrappy string quilts. Simple quilting is recommended.

Stippling

Stippling is a simple, random, allover quilt design.

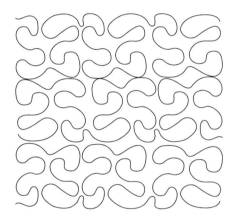

Waves in One Direction

Gentle curving lines that are relatively easy to accomplish with a walking foot. This is a nice design and a simple quilting technique.

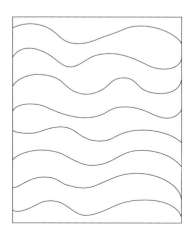

Waves in Both Directions

Quilting waves in both directions creates an interesting grid-like quilting design. It is denser than the single wave design.

BINDING

Binding provides a line around the edge of your quilt and is the final design element.

Single Fabric

Using a single fabric adds a prominent thin line around the edge of the quilt. The It's a Jolly Holiday quilt on page 68 uses a single fabric binding.

Disappearing

A binding that disappears into the quilt background or border is another option. The black binding on the String Circles quilt on page 118 is the same fabric as the background so the binding disappears.

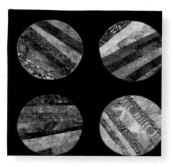

Scrappy

Since most of the string quilt projects are scrappy, a scrappy binding is often the perfect choice. Use several fabrics from the quilt center for the binding. A sample of quilts with scrappy bindings is shown.

String Piecing Techniques

String piecing is relatively easy and provides a break from detailed piecing. Since the fabric strings are sewn to a foundation and then trimmed, precise sewing is not as crucial as when stitching pieced blocks. While you can use precut strips, string quilts typically utilize fabric you already have and use a wide variety of string widths.

In this section you will learn to make a variety of string pieced blocks. The strings in the projects range in width from 1" to 2-½" with more strings in the 1-¼" to 1-¾" range. For blocks smaller than 6-½" the strings should generally be less than 2"-wide. A variety of lengths are needed so don't discard the shorter strings. These can be used in corners or as disappearing strings.

PREPARING AND CUTTING STRINGS

Cutting fabric strings is easy. Any fabric left over from another project or your stash can be cut into varying widths of fabric strings and set aside for a string quilt. Toss strings in a bin or bag. Do not try to keep them separated by width. Some projects do require specific sized strings, so if you have a project in mind, check the instructions before cutting your strings.

1. Press the fabrics before cutting. Place the fabric on a cutting mat and using a ruler, measure in approximately 2"-2-½" from the raw edge. There is no need to square up the fabric, even if the ends do not match. Using a rotary cutter cut the first string. The crooked string will be used in the same manner as a straight string.

Adding Selvages

Selvages can add a unique touch to a string quilt. To incorporate selvages into your quilt, line up a ruler on the selvage edge and cut a 1-½"-wide strip. This will give you the selvage, as well as some of the fabric.

2. Continue cutting strings in a variety of widths.

3. Leftover fabric scraps can be used to cut crooked or angled strings.

Mary's Tips: Making Blocks
- Shorten stitch length
- String edges should cover foundation
- Press strings flat before adding more; prevents bubbles
- Keep short strings separate; use in corners

BUILDING DIAGONAL STRING BLOCKS

The majority of projects in this book are made with diagonal string blocks. They are easy to make by covering a square foundation diagonally with strings.

1. Cut the foundations to the size needed. Place a fabric string, right side up, at the diagonal center of the foundation. Make sure the string is covering the corners of the foundation. Place a few pins along the left edge of the string where they will not interfere with sewing the next string. With experience it may not be necessary to pin the center strip.

2. Place another fabric string on the first, right sides together and matching right raw edges. The second fabric string should be long enough to cover the foundation edges when pressed open. Pin the string in place and sew along the right edge.

3. Remove all pins and finger press open.

4. In the same manner, place a fabric string on the center strip, right sides together and matching left raw edges. The string should cover the foundation edges when pressed open. Pin the string in place and sew along the left edge. Remove the pins and press open.

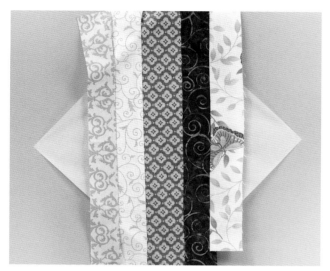

5. Continue sewing strings to the foundation. Placing a string on each side and then sewing will save time. Press well after adding each set of strings.

6. Continue adding strings until the foundation is covered.

TRIMMING STRING BLOCKS

After the foundation is completely covered with strings you can trim the block.

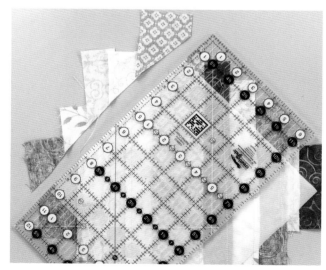

1. Place the block right side down on a cutting mat. The foundation should be facing up.

2. Place the ruler on one edge of the foundation and trim.

3. Continue trimming each edge of the foundation to complete the string block.

TRIMMING ROUGH-CUT FOUNDATION BLOCKS

Rough-cut, or oversized foundations are a bit larger than the exact size of the unfinished block. They need to be trimmed to the correct size after being sewn. Instead of using the foundation edges as a cutting guide, the blocks are trimmed using a square ruler or whatever you normally use to square up blocks. A small rotating cutting mat is also useful. An AccuQuilt!® cutter may be used if the correct size is available.

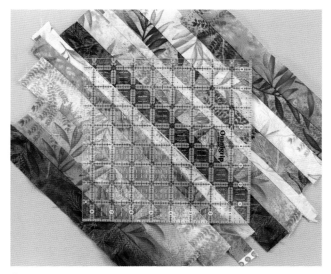

1. Place the desired size ruler on the front of the string block.

2. Trim around the ruler on all sides to complete the string block.

REMOVING FOUNDATIONS

Unless you have used a permanent foundation, it will need to be removed after the block is trimmed. They are relatively easy to remove since stitching the strings perforates the foundation. Use a pencil, knitting needle, seam ripper or chopstick to help loosen the foundation. A bent tweezers is also handy for grabbing small bits of paper.

1. Fold down one corner of the foundation and tear it away.

2. Loosen the top of the next section using one of the items mentioned above. A small, narrow tool works best to get close to the stitching without pulling it out.

3. Fold that section down and tear it away.

4. Continue in the same manner until the foundation has been removed. Remove any extra bits of foundation with a bent tweezers.

ADDING INTEREST AND VARIATION TO STRING BLOCKS

Changing the width of strings, incorporating crooked or skinny strings and varying the value, print and color of fabric adds variety and interest to the blocks. Crooked, disappearing and selvage strings all add a wonky or irregular element to diagonal string blocks.

Adding Crooked Strings

Crooked strings can be added anywhere in the string block and in any number. Place them in the center of the block or on each side; add several or just one. Experiment and have fun.

1. Referring to Building Diagonal String Blocks on pages 33-34, sew the first two strings to the foundation. Place a fabric string at an angle on one of the sewn strings, right sides together.

2. Sew the string in place. Turn the foundation paper under the block and out of the way. Trim the excess seam allowance. with a rotary cutter or scissors.

3. Fold the foundation paper back in place and press to reveal a crooked string.

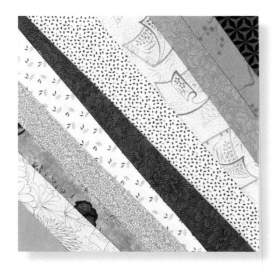

4. Continue adding strings until the foundation is covered. Trim the block to size and remove the foundation paper.

Adding Disappearing Strings

Scraps of fabric are perfect for making disappearing strings. These strings do not go all the way across the block and are another way to add interest and variety.

1. Referring to Building Diagonal String Blocks on pages 33-34, sew the first two strings to the foundation.

2. Place a fabric scrap or crooked string on one of the sewn strings, right sides together.

3. Sew the string in place and press open.

4. Continue adding strings until the foundation is covered. Trim the block to size and remove the foundation paper.

Adding Selvage Strings

Selvage strings are incorporated into many of the projects in this book. Cut selvages at least 1-1/2"-wide. This will give you the selvage as well as some of the colored or printed part of the fabric.

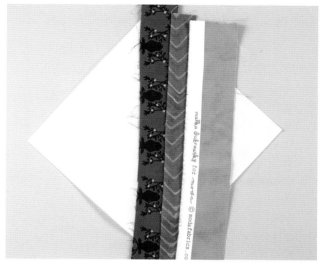

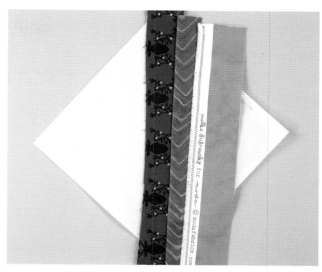

1. To add a selvage string, place it right side up on one of the previously sewn strings overlapping the previous string by approximately 1/4". Pin the selvage in place.

2. Using a narrow zigzag stitch, sew the strings together where they overlap. Sew as close to the selvage edge as possible. This will prevent any loose selvage edges from getting caught or tucked under during the quilting process. If you prefer, you can use a wide zigzag or straight stitch.

Note: A contrasting thread was used for illustration purposes.

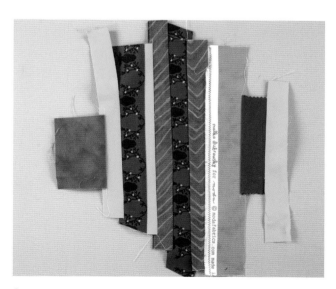

3. Continue adding strings until the foundation is covered.

4. Trim the block to size and remove the foundation paper.

STRING PLACEMENT

String placement plays an important role when you are working to achieve a specific design. For example, Uncle Ernie's Rocker quilt on page 64 uses one dark and one light string centered on the foundation. Dark strings are then sewn to one side and light strings to the other to achieve a diamond design within the quilt. Other designs, such as the Juggling Summer quilt on page 102, require exact placement of a single string in a specific size.

Centering One String in a Block

To center one string on the foundation, mark a line one half the measurement of the string you are centering.

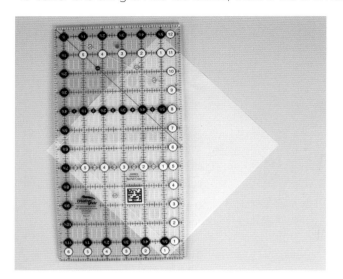

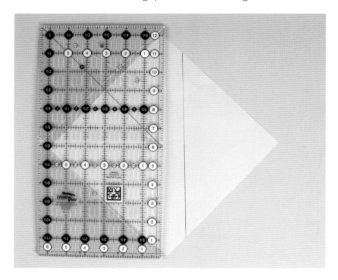

1. Place a ruler on the foundation with the 1" mark on the diagonal center. The 1" line on the ruler should go through the foundation's two corners.

Note: The example shown uses a 2" center string, which means a line needs to be drawn 1" from the foundation's center. If using a different size string, mark a line one half the measurement of the string you are centering.

2. Using a pencil, draw a line on the foundation as shown.

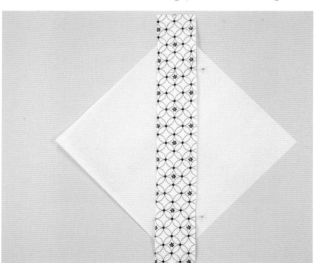

3. Place a string right side up on the foundation with one raw edge on the marked line. Make sure the string covers both corners of the foundation. Use a few pins to hold the string in place.

4. Place the second string right side down on the first string with one raw edge on the drawn line. Use a few pins to hold the string in place.

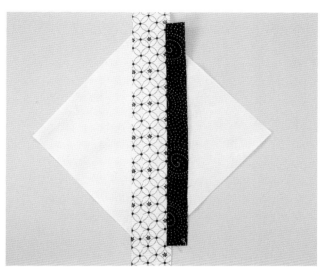

5. Using a ¼" seam allowance, sew the strings together along the right edge. Remove the pins and press open.

6. In the same manner, sew the next string on the oppostie side of the center string. Press open.

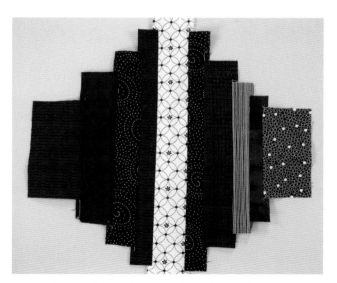

7. Continue adding strings until the foundation is covered.

8. Trim the block to size and remove the foundation paper.

Centering Two Strings in a Block

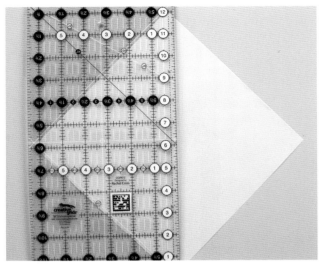

1. Place a ruler on the foundation with the ¼" mark on the diagonal center. The ¼" line on the ruler should go through the foundation's two corners.

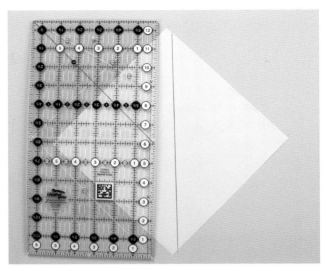

2. Using a pencil, draw a line on the foundation as shown. The raw edges of the first two strings will be placed on the drawn line and then sewn. This will ensure the seam is at the diagonal center of the foundation.

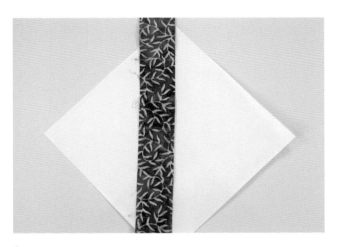

3. Place a string right side up on the foundation with one raw edge on the marked line. Make sure the string covers both corners of the foundation. Smooth out the string and use a few pins to hold it in place along the drawn line if desired.

4. Place the second string right side down on the first string with one raw edge on the drawn line. Use a few pins to hold the string in place.

5. Using a ¼" seam allowance, sew the strings together along the right edge. Remove the pins and press the strings open. Flip the foundation over. The stitch line should go directly through two corners of the foundation, which ensures the two strings are exactly in the center of the block.

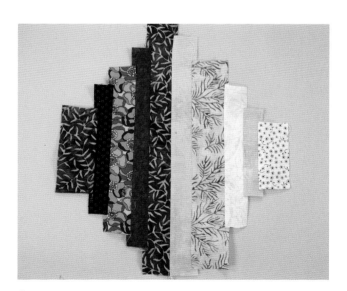

6. Continue adding strings until the foundation is covered.

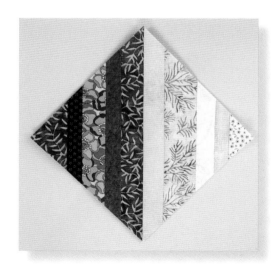

7. Trim the block to size and remove the foundation paper.

Making Diamonds

Four rectangular foundations are needed to create the diamond shape shown. Light and dark value strings are sewn to opposite sides of each foundation. Two foundations will need the light strings on the right and two will need the light strings on the left. When the blocks are sewn together they will create the diamond shape.

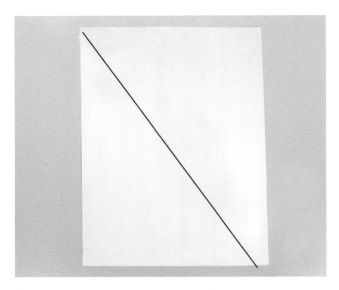

1. Draw a line on the foundation a ¼" from the diagonal center as shown.

Note: For exact string placement, refer to Centering Two Strings in a Block on pages 42-43.

2. Place a dark value fabric string, right side up, at the diagonal center of the rectangular foundation. Make sure the string extends past the foundation's corners.

3. Place a light string, right side down, on the dark string aligning raw edges to be sewn.

4. Sew the string in place and press open.

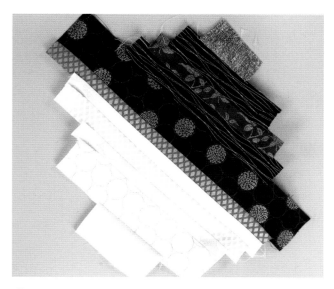

5. Continue adding light strings to one side of the foundation and dark strings to the other until the foundation is covered. Trim the block to size and remove the foundation. Make two blocks with the light strings on the left.

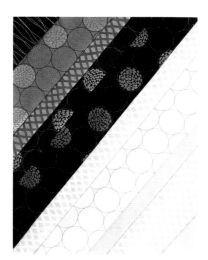

6. Make two blocks with the light strings on the right.

7. Referring to Sewing String Blocks Together on page 57 and Four-Block Diamond Design on page 18, sew the four blocks together to make a diamond block.

BUILDING STRING BLOCKS WITH SHAPES

Triangles, diamonds and circles are a few of the shapes that can be incorporated into string blocks. These blocks are created using solid fabric shapes, fabric foundations or foundations cut into various shapes.

Making Floating Triangles

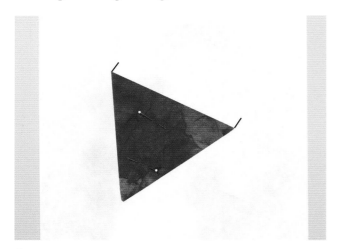

1. Cut a fabric triangle the desired size and place it right side up on the foundation. Use a few pins to hold the triangle in place. Mark the foundation at the points of the triangle to show where to start and stop sewing.

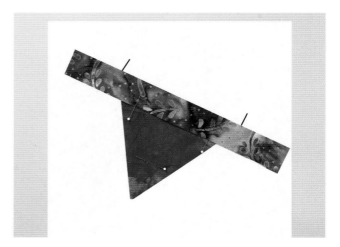

2. Choose a fabric string that will extend past the edge of the triangle. This string will be trimmed even with the triangle edge so it is important that it is long enough. Place the chosen string, right side down, on the triangle's edge. Pin in place.

3. Sew the pieces together beginning at one pencil mark and continuing to the next. Press the string open.

4. Fold the foundation back and use a ruler and rotary cutter to trim the fabric string even with the triangle. Take care not to cut the foundation.

Mary's Tip
If you have sewn too far to easily fold the foundation back, use a seam ripper to loosen some stitches.

5. In the same manner, trim the other side of the string even with the triangle.
Using a pencil, mark the foundation at the points of the triangle and the trimmed string to show where to start and stop sewing.

6. Place another string, right side down, on the triangle's edge. Sew the pieces together beginning at one pencil mark and continuing to the next. Press the string open.

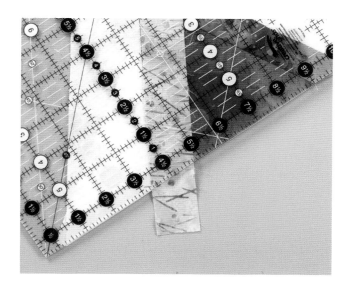

7. Fold the foundation back and use a ruler and rotary cutter to trim the fabric string even with the triangle. Take care not to cut the foundation.

8. Trim the remaining side of the string even with the triangle. Continue adding strings around the triangle until the foundation is covered. The strings do not require trimming if they go off the edge of the foundation.

9. Trim the block to size and remove the foundation paper.

Think Like a Designer

Collect design ideas by...

- keeping a notebook or album on your phone or computer
- diagraming, doodling and taking photos
- looking in magazines and online
- finding shapes and designs you like
- testing ideas to see what works

Mary's Musings

I pause periodically during design and construction to ask myself...

- do I have unifying elements?
- do I have enough variety?
- do I have too much variety?
- are the colors working?
- are the proportions correct?

This allows me to reevaluate my design and make any needed changes.

Making Single Half-Square Triangles

Single half-square triangles are constructed on one half of a foundation. The remaining foundation is cut away when the triangle is trimmed. Single half-square triangles are used as setting triangles in the Solid Squares quilt on page 112.

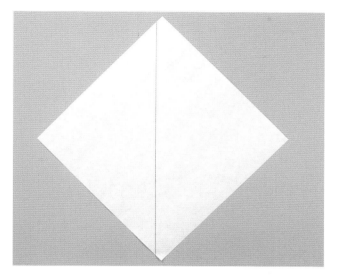

1. Using a pencil, draw a line ¼" from the center of the foundation square.

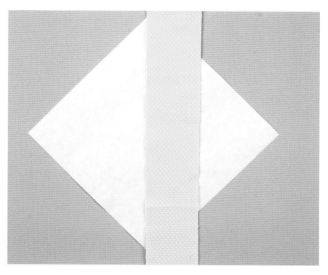

2. Place a fabric string on the foundation, right side up, with a raw edge of the string aligned with the marked line. You will be sewing strings to only one side of the foundation.

3. Place another string, right side down, on the first string with the raw edges to be sewn lined up as shown. Sew the string in place and press open.

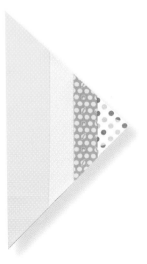

4. Continue adding strings to one half of the foundation until it is covered. Trim the half-square triangle to size and remove the foundation paper.

Making Two Half-Square Triangles on a Single Block

These blocks are made with one half-square triangle that is a single fabric while the other half is covered with strings. The Selvage Pinwheels quilt on page 92 uses these blocks in its design.

1. Using a pencil, draw a line ¼" from the center of the foundation square.

2. Place an oversize triangle on the drawn line, right side up, as shown.

Note: For an 8-½" foundation, cut a 9-½" fabric square. Cut the square in half diagonally to make the oversize triangle.

3. Place a string, right side down, on the oversize triangle aligning the raw edges to be sewn.

4. Sew the string in place and press open.

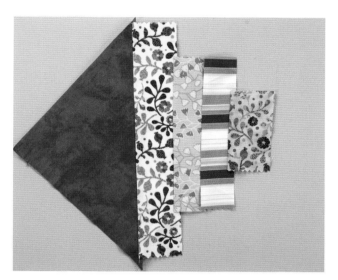

5. Continue adding strings until the foundation is covered.

6. Trim the block to size and remove the foundation paper.

Mary's Musings

Sometimes if an idea isn't quite working I will simplify the design by removing some of the elements or colors. Then I can gradually add things back in as needed.

Mary's Tip

When you have small leftover pieces of fabric cut them into crooked strings for future projects.

Making Half-Square Triangles with Perpendicular Strings

Blocks constructed with half-square triangle sections consisting of perpendicular strings create interesting designs. Try using strings in variations of one color on each side or randomly choose strings from your scrap bag to make the blocks.

1. Using a pencil, draw a line ¼" from the center of the foundation square.

2. Referring to the photo, center a string right side up and perpendicular to the line drawn on the foundation. The string should extend past the drawn line and the foundation corner.

3. Place another string, right side down, on the first string aligning the raw edges to be sewn. The second string should also extend past the drawn line and the foundation.

4. Sew the string in place and press open.

5. Continue adding strings until one half of the foundation is covered.

6. Referring to the photo, place a string right side down over the edges of the sewn strings. The string needs to be long enough to cover the edges of all the strings and extend past the corners of the foundation.

7. Sew the string in place and press open.

8. Place another string, right side down, on the previous string aligning raw edges to be sewn. The string should extend past the foundation when pressed open.

9. Sew the string in place and press open.

10. Continue adding strings until the foundation is covered.

11. Trim the block to size and remove the foundation paper.

Think Like a Designer

Design with half-square triangles with perpendicular strings by...

- covering half with dark strings and half with light strings
- using different color combinations on each side of the block
- experimenting to see what designs you can create

String Quilt Projects

My Blue Heaven Quilt

Finished quilt size approximately: 80" X 80"
Finished block size: 8"

Quilting design by Mary M. Hogan; quilted by Mary M. Hogan and Yessant Habetz.

A bundle of beautiful blue fabrics combined with a search through my stash became the starting point for the My Blue Heaven quilt. I experimented with many fabrics for the center strings before settling on a bright green.

MATERIALS

- (100) 8-½" square foundations
- 1-⅝ yards green print fabric for center strings
- 10 yards assorted blue prints, solids and selvages for blocks
- Scraps of green fabrics for the focal block
- ¾ yard binding fabric
- 7-½ yards backing fabric

Note: Fabric requirements may vary depending on the width and placement of strings.

wof = width of fabric

Fabric is 42"-44"-wide unless otherwise noted.

Read through String Piecing Techniques on pages 32-57 before beginning.

CUTTING INSTRUCTIONS

From green print fabric, cut:

(33) 1-¾" x wof strips. From each strip, cut:
(3) 1-¾" x 14" strings for a total of (102) strings

Note: You will need 99 for the center strings.

From the remaining fabric, cut:
1" - 2-½" strings for the green block
Cut more 1-¼" - 1-¾" strings than other strings.

From assorted blue prints and solids, cut:

1-½" selvage strings

A range of 1" - 2-½" x wof strings
Cut more 1-¼" - 1-¾" strings than other strings.

From scraps of green fabrics, cut:

A range of 1" - 2-½" x wof strings
Cut more 1-¼" - 1-¾" strings than other strings.

From backing fabric cut:

(3) 90" lengthwise pieces

From binding fabric, cut:

(10) 2-½" x wof strips
Note: The featured quilt was bound with 2 green and 8 blue strips.

DESIGN ELEMENTS

Focal point	• green square with blue center
	• green center strings
Unifying elements	• same width green string in diagonal center of blue blocks
Variation	• blue fabrics
	• width of strings
	• selvages add bright white
	• 2 different fabrics for binding
	• green block with blue center
Color	• blue
	• green
Line and shape	• blocks oriented in same direction create diagonal lines across quilt

CONSTRUCTING THE BLOCKS

1. Place a green center string, right side up, near the diagonal center of a foundation square.

2. Lay an assorted blue string right side down on the green string, matching the raw edges to be sewn. Secure with pins if desired.

3. Sew the strings together using a ¼" seam. Press the string open.

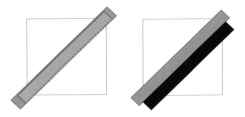

4. Continue sewing blue strings on either side of the green string until the foundation is covered to complete a blue block. Make a total of 99 blue blocks.

Make 99

5. Place a 1-¾" blue string near the center of the remaining foundation square. Referring to steps 2-4, sew green strings on either side of the blue string to make 1 green block.

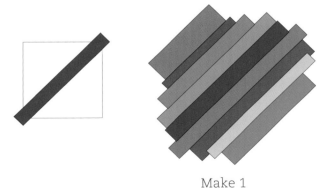

Make 1

PREPARING BLOCKS FOR QUILT TOP ASSEMBLY

1. Press blocks carefully, using starch if needed to stabilize the blocks.

2. Trim blocks to 8-½" square.

3. Remove the foundation papers.

QUILT TOP ASSEMBLY

1. Sew the string blocks together in 25 sets of 4. Include the green block in one of the sets.

Note: When sewing diagonally pieced blocks together, use a ¼" seam allowance. Press seams open.

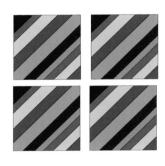 

Make 25 sets

2. Referring to the Quilt Top Assembly Diagram, lay out the 4-block sets in 5 rows with 5 sets in each row.

3. Sew the block sets together in rows. Press seams open. Sew the rows together to complete the quilt top.

Quilt Top Assembly Diagram

FINISHING THE QUILT

1. Sew the 3 backing pieces together as shown. Press seams open.

2. Layer the backing, batting and quilt top together and baste. Quilt as desired.

3. Sew the binding strips together using diagonal seams to create one continuous strip. Press the strip in half lengthwise, wrong sides together, and sew to the raw edge of the quilt top. Fold binding over raw edges and hand stitch in place.

Note: Leftover blocks don't need to go to waste. Sew them together in a column and use the column as a design element on the back of your quilt.

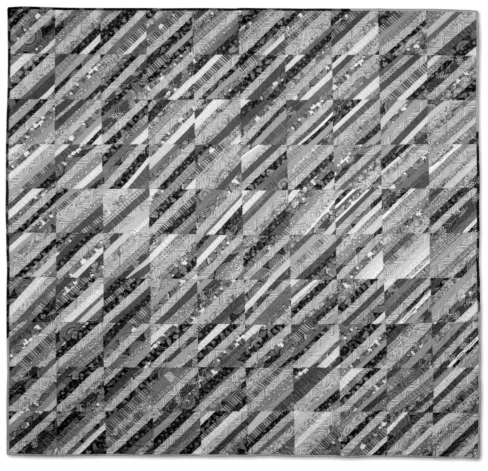

My Blue Heaven Quilt
80" X 80"

Uncle Ernie's Rocker Quilt

Finished quilt size approximately: 80" x 90"
Finished block size: 10"

Some cuts of Civil War reproduction fabrics had been languishing in a box at my home quilting store, The Quilting Season. Mary, the owner, suggested I take them and "do something with them." This was an opportunity for me to use a very different fabric style. This quilt is named after a rocking chair in the store that had belonged to the owner's Uncle Ernie.

MATERIALS

- (72) 10-½" square foundations
- 1-½ yards dark fabric for center strings
- 1-½ yards light fabric for center strings
- 5 yards assorted light fabrics for strings
- 5 yards assorted dark fabric for strings
- ¾ yard binding fabric
- 7-½ yards backing fabric

Note: Fabric requirements may vary depending on the width and placement of strings.

wof = width of fabric

Fabric is 42"-44"-wide unless otherwise noted.

Read through String Piecing Techniques on pages 32-57 before beginning.

DESIGN ELEMENTS

Focal point	• dark center square
Unifying elements	• consistent use of light and dark value fabrics
	• center string fabric
	• center string width
Variation	• fabric
	• width of strings
Color	• browns, beige, blue, red
Fabric style	• Civil War reproduction
Line and shape	• squares radiating around center focal block

CUTTING INSTRUCTIONS

From dark center string fabric, cut:

(3) 15-½" x wof strips. From the strips, cut:
(72) 1-½" x 15-½" strings

Cut any remaining fabric into 1" - 2-½" strings

From light center string fabric, cut:

(3) 15-½" x wof strips. From the strips, cut:
(72) 1-½" x 15-½" strings

Cut any remaining fabric into 1" - 2-½" strings

From assorted light fabrics, cut:

1-½" selvage strings

A range of 1" - 2-½" x wof strips
Cut more 1" - 2" strings than other sizes.

From assorted dark fabrics, cut:

1-½" selvage strings

A range of 1" - 2-½" x wof strips
Cut more 1" - 2" strings than other sizes.

From backing fabric, cut:

(3) 90" lengthwise pieces

From binding fabric, cut:

(10) 2-½" x wof strips

CONSTRUCTING THE BLOCKS

Note: The two center strings, one light and one dark, are placed so their seam is at the diagonal center of the block. Refer to Centering Two Strings in a Block on page 42.

1. Draw a diagonal line ¼" from the center of a foundation block.

2. Place a 1-½" - 15-½" light center string right side up on the foundation block, matching a raw edge of the string and the drawn line. Lay a 1-½" - 15-½" dark center string right side down on the light string, matching the raw edges to be sewn. Secure with pins if desired.

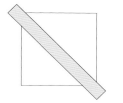

3. Sew the strings together using a ¼" seam. Press the string open.

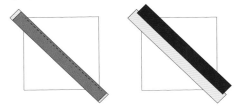

4. Continue adding light strings to the light center string and dark strings to the dark center string. Sew a variety of string widths and fabrics within each block.

5. Cover the foundation to complete a block. Make a total of 72 blocks.

Make 72

PREPARING BLOCKS FOR QUILT TOP ASSEMBLY

1. Press blocks carefully, using starch if needed to stabilize the blocks.

2. Trim blocks to 10-½" square.

3. Remove the foundation papers.

QUILT TOP ASSEMBLY

1. Referring to the Quilt Top Assembly Diagram, lay out the blocks in 9 rows with 8 blocks in each row. Pay close attention to the orientation of the blocks.

2. Sew the blocks together in rows. Press seams open.

Note: When sewing diagonally pieced blocks together, use a ¼" seam allowance.

3. Sew the rows together to complete the quilt top.

Quilt Top Assembly Diagram

FINISHING THE QUILT

1. Sew the 3 backing pieces together as shown. Press seams open.

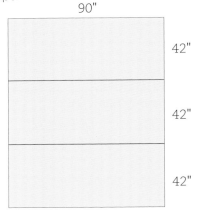

2. Layer the backing, batting and quilt top together and baste. Quilt as desired.

3. Sew the binding strips together using diagonal seams to create one continuous strip. Press the strip in half lengthwise, wrong sides together, and sew to the raw edge of the quilt top. Fold binding over raw edges and hand stitch in place.

Uncle Ernie's Rocker Quilt
80" x 90"

It's a Jolly Holiday Quilt

Finished quilt size approximately: 68" x 84"
Finished block size: 8"

It's a Jolly Holiday quilt is the perfect opportunity to use up the holiday fabric languishing in your stash. Add some coordinating solids and stripes for more visual interest. The idea for the focal point came after reading *Quilting Modern* by Jacqui Gering and Karen Pedersen.

MATERIALS

- (80) 8-½" square foundations
- 2-¼ yards solid red fabric for blocks and borders
- 6 yards assorted holiday fabric for blocks
- 3 yards assorted coordinating prints and solids for blocks
- ¾ yard stripe fabric for binding
- 5 yards backing fabric

Note: Fabric requirements may vary depending on the width and placement of strings.

wof = width of fabric

Fabric is 42"-44"-wide unless otherwise noted.

Read through String Piecing Techniques on pages 32-57 before beginning.

DESIGN ELEMENTS

Focal point	• irregular red square
Unifying elements	• red string in majority of blocks
	• holiday fabrics and limited color scheme
Variation	• fabric
	• width of strings
Color	• red, blue, green and white
	• red is darkest value
Line and shape	• blocks oriented around focal block

CUTTING INSTRUCTIONS

From solid red fabric, cut:

(2) 5" squares. Cut the squares in half on the diagonal to make 4 half-square triangles

(8) 2-½" border strips

Cut any remaining fabric into 1" – 2-½" strings

From assorted holiday and coordinating print and solid fabrics, cut:

1-½" selvage strings

A range of 1" – 2-½" x wof strings

Cut more 1-¼" - 1-¾" strings than other strings.

From backing fabric cut

(2) 90" lengthwise pieces

From stripe fabric, cut:

(8) 2-½" x wof binding strips

CONSTRUCTING THE BLOCKS

1. Place an assorted holiday or solid fabric string, right side up, near the center of a foundation square.

2. Lay another string right side down on the first string, matching the raw edges to be sewn. Secure with pins if desired.

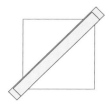

3. Sew the strings together using a ¼" seam. Press the string open.

4. Continue adding strings to the foundation. Cover one corner of the foundation with a red half-square triangle to complete a focus block. Make 4 focus blocks.

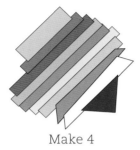

Make 4

5. Repeat to make 76 blocks using the remaining strings and foundation squares.

Note: In the featured quilt, a majority of the blocks have a solid red string.

Make 76

PREPARING BLOCKS FOR QUILT TOP ASSEMBLY

1. Press blocks carefully. Use starch if needed to stabilize the blocks.

2. Trim blocks to 8-½" square.

3. Remove the foundation papers.

QUILT CENTER ASSEMBLY

1. Referring to the Quilt Center Assembly Diagram, lay out the blocks in 10 rows with 8 blocks in each row. Pay close attention to the placement of the focus blocks and the orientation of all the blocks.

2. Sew the blocks together in rows. Press seams open.

Note: When sewing diagonally pieced blocks together, use a ¼" seam allowance. Press seams open.

3. Sew the rows together to complete the quilt top.

Quilt Center Assembly Diagram

ADDING THE BORDERS

1. Sew the 2-½" solid red border strips together end to end to make one strip.

2. Measure the quilt center from top to bottom and cut 2 border strips to this size. Sew the strips to opposite sides of the quilt center. Press seams toward the border.

3. Measure the quilt center from side to side and cut 2 border strips to this size. Sew the strips to the top and bottom of the quilt center. Press seams toward the border.

FINISHING THE QUILT

1. Sew the 2 backing pieces together as shown. Press seams open.

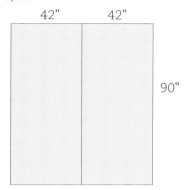

2. Layer the backing, batting and quilt top together and baste. Quilt as desired.

3. Sew the binding strips together using diagonal seams to create one continuous strip. Press the strip in half lengthwise, wrong sides together, and sew to the raw edge of the quilt top. Fold binding over raw edges and hand stitch in place.

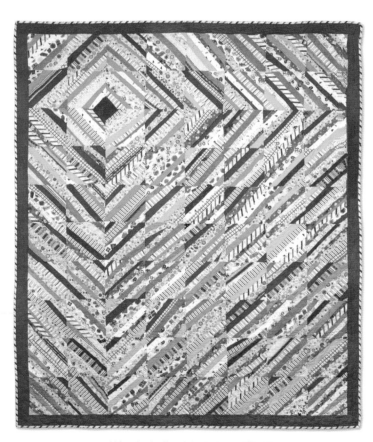

It's A Jolly Holiday Quilt
68" x 84"

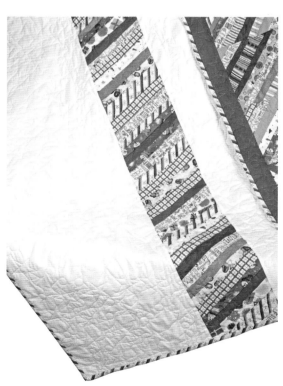

Note: Leftover strips are sewn into a column and sewn between solid white fabric pieces to create the quilt back for the It's A Jolly Holiday quilt.

Birds in the Woods Quilt

Finished quilt size approximately: 80" x 96"

Finished block size: 8"

A group of fabrics featuring birds and leaves inspired the Birds in the Woods quilt. Primitive-looking birds are raw-edge appliquéd over the quilt top. The lighter value blocks represent a clearing in the woods.

MATERIALS

- (120) 8-½" square foundations
- 8 yards assorted light and dark print fabrics for blocks
- 4 yards assorted light and dark solid fabrics for blocks
- ½ yard assorted yellow print and solid fabrics for blocks
- ¾ yard dark brown fabric for bird body and leg appliqués
- ⅛ yard light brown fabric for bird wing appliqué
- ¾ yard binding fabric
- 6-¾ yards backing fabric
- 2 yards Heat N Bond® Lite or other fusible product for appliqué
- Appliqué patterns on page 77

Note: Fabric requirements may vary depending on the width and placement of strings.

wof = width of fabric

Fabric is 42"-44"-wide unless otherwise noted.

Read through String Piecing Techniques on pages 32-57 before beginning.

CUTTING INSTRUCTIONS

Note: Decide on your string width preference before cutting all the print and solid fabrics into strings.

From *all* assorted print fabrics, cut:

1-½" selvage strings

From *all* assorted print and solid fabrics, cut:

A range of 1" - 2-½" x wof strings

Cut more 1-¼" - 1-¾" strings than other strings.

From backing fabric, cut:

(2) 104" x wof pieces

(3) 9" x wof pieces

From binding fabric, cut:

(10) 2-½" x wof strips

DESIGN ELEMENTS

Focal point	• light value 16-block area with bird appliqué
Unifying elements	• bird, leaf and plant fabrics
	• bird appliqués
Variation	• fabric, width of strings
	• birds appliquéd at different angles with varying wing positions
Color	• light and dark values with yellow accents
Line and shape	• square block setting

CONSTRUCTING THE BLOCKS

1. Place an assorted light string, right side up, near the diagonal center of a foundation square.

2. Lay another light string right side down on the first string, matching the raw edges to be sewn. Secure with pins if desired.

3. Sew the strings together using a ¼" seam. Press the string open.

4. Continue adding assorted light strings to either side of the center string. Sew a variety of string widths and angles within each block. Use an occasional selvage or yellow string as well.

5. Cover the foundation to complete a light string block. Make 16 light string blocks.

Make 16

6. Repeat to make 104 blocks using a combination of light and dark strings.

Make 104

PREPARING BLOCKS FOR QUILT TOP ASSEMBLY

1. Press blocks carefully. Use starch if needed to stabilize the blocks.

2. Trim blocks to 8-½" square.

3. Remove the foundation papers.

SEW BLOCK SETS TOGETHER

1. Sew the 16 light string blocks together as shown to make a 16-block set. Note the orientation of the blocks.

Note: When sewing diagonally pieced blocks together, use a ¼" seam allowance. Press seams open.

2. Sew the remaining string blocks together in 26 sets of 4.

 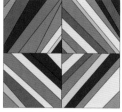

Make 26 sets

ADDING THE APPLIQUÉ

Note: In the featured quilt, the birds were cut with a pinking shears and raw-edge appliquéd to the 4-block and 16-block sets.

1. Trace the bird body, wing and leg patterns on page 77 onto the paper side of the fusible. Trace the patterns in the numbers given.

16—Bird Body

17—Bird Body Reversed

16—Wing

17—Wing Reversed

66 (33 of each)—Leg

2. Cut out the shapes leaving approximately ¼" of fusible beyond the outside of each shape.

3. Following the manufacturer's instructions, fuse the shapes to the wrong side of the dark and light brown appliqué fabrics. Cut out the shapes on the traced lines. Remove the paper backing from each shape.

4. Referring to the photo on page 76, position the bird body, wing and leg shapes to the 16-block set and the 4-block sets. Fuse in place, following manufacturer's instructions.

5. Using a small zigzag or straight stitch, sew between ⅛" - ¼" from the edge of the appliqué pieces. A straight stitch was used to sew down the center of each bird leg.

QUILT TOP ASSEMBLY

1. Referring to the Quilt Top Assembly Diagram, lay out the 16-block and 4-block sets as shown.

2. Sew the block sets together in rows. Press seams open. To complete the row with the 16-block set, sew (4) 4-block sets together and (2) 4-block sets together. Sew these sets to either side of the 16-block set to complete the row.

Note: When sewing diagonally pieced blocks together, use a ¼" seam allowance. Press seams open.

3. Sew the rows together to complete the quilt top.

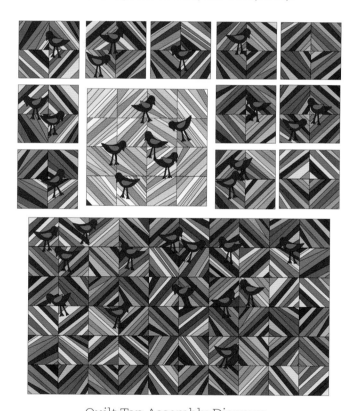

Quilt Top Assembly Diagram

FINISHING THE QUILT

1. Sew the (3) 9" x wof backing pieces together end to end to make a 9" x 126" piece.

2. Sew the (2) 104" x wof backing pieces to either side of the 9" x 126" piece. Press seams open.

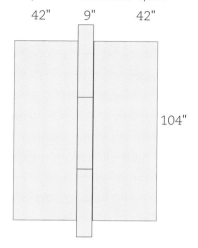

3. Trim away any excess length.

4. Layer the backing, batting and quilt top together and baste. Quilt as desired.

5. Sew the binding strips together using diagonal seams to create one continuous strip. Press the strip in half lengthwise, wrong sides together, and sew to the raw edge of the quilt top. Fold binding over raw edges and hand stitch in place.

Birds in the Woods Quilt
80" x 96"

BIRD TEMPLATES

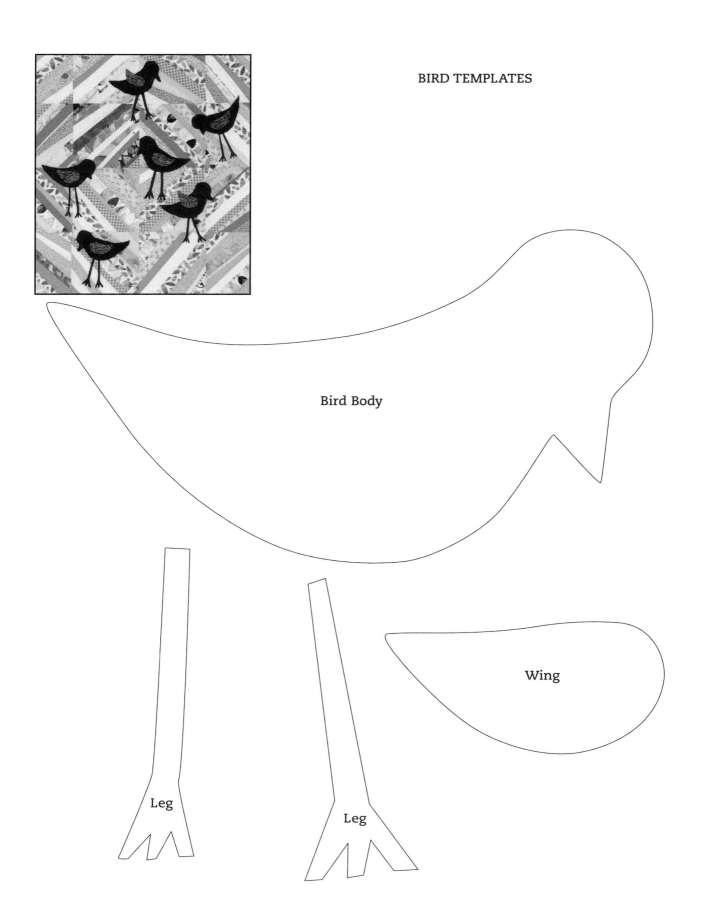

Bird Body

Wing

Leg

Leg

In the Summertime Coverlet

Finished quilt size approximately: 80" X 96"
Finished block size: 8"

The In the Summertime Coverlet was inspired by a block of the month project using 1930's reproduction prints. Instead of making the suggested blocks, I used the fabric for a string quilt with muslin foundation squares. Prints, solids and selvages happily coexist in this project. White and purple are included in each block and purple binding finishes the quilt.

MATERIALS

- 7-¼ yards muslin fabric for foundations
- 10 yards assorted 1930's reproduction prints and light solid fabrics for blocks
- 2 yards white solid fabric for blocks
- 2 yards assorted purple solid and print fabrics for blocks
- ¾ yard binding fabric
- 6-⅝ yards backing fabric

Note: Fabric requirements may vary depending on the width and placement of strings.

wof = width of fabric

Fabric is 42"-44"-wide unless otherwise noted.

Read through String Piecing Techniques on pages 32-57 before beginning.

DESIGN ELEMENTS

Unifying elements	• 1930's fabrics
	• white and purple in each block
Variation	• assorted fabrics
	• width of strings
	• selvages add bright white to blocks
Color	• primarily light value
Line and shape	• blocks oriented to suggest on point squares

CUTTING INSTRUCTIONS

Note: Decide on your string width preference before cutting all the print and solid fabrics into strings.

From muslin fabric, cut:

(30) 8-½" x wof strips. From each strip, cut:
(4) 8-½" squares for a total of 120 muslin foundation squares

From *all* assorted print fabrics, cut:

1-½" selvage strings

From *all* assorted print and solid fabrics, cut:

A range of 1" - 2-½" x wof strings
Cut more 1-¼" - 1-¾" strings than other sizes.

From backing fabric, cut:

(2) 104" x wof pieces

(3) 9" x wof pieces

From binding fabric, cut:

(10) 2-½" x wof strips

Note: The featured quilt uses 4 assorted purple fabrics for the binding.

Tips for using muslin foundation squares

- Use a walking foot to keep the fabric and foundation from shifting
- Sew in the same direction each time you add a string

CONSTRUCTING THE BLOCKS

1. Place a string, right side up, near the diagonal center of a foundation square.

2. Lay another string right side down on the first string, matching the raw edges to be sewn. Secure with pins if desired.

3. Sew the strings together using a ¼" seam. Press the string open.

4. Continue sewing strings on either side of the first string. Include at least one purple solid or print and one white solid string in each block. These can be placed in any position. Sew a variety of string widths and angles within each block. Use an occasional selvage string as well.

5. Cover the foundation to complete a block. Make a total of 120 blocks.

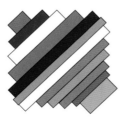

Make 120

PREPARING BLOCKS FOR QUILT TOP ASSEMBLY

1. Press blocks carefully, using starch if needed to stabilize the blocks.

2. Trim blocks to 8-½" square.

3. Do not remove the muslin foundations.

QUILT TOP ASSEMBLY

1. Sew the string blocks together in 30 sets of 4.

Note: When sewing diagonally pieced blocks together, use a ¼" seam allowance. Press seams open.

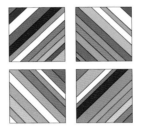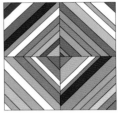

Make 30 sets

2. Referring to the Quilt Top Assembly Diagram, lay out the 4-block sets in 6 rows with 5 sets in each row.

3. Sew the block sets together in rows. Press seams open. Sew the rows together to complete the quilt top.

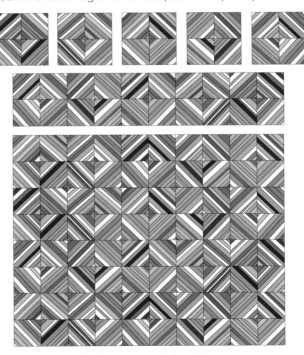

Quilt Top Assembly Diagram

FINISHING THE QUILT

1. Sew the (3) 9" x wof backing pieces together end to end to make a 9" x 126" piece.

2. Sew the (2) 104" x wof backing pieces to either side of the 9" x 126" piece. Press seams open.

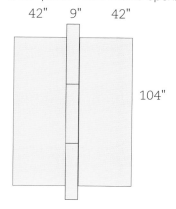

42"   9"   42"

104"

3. Trim away any excess length.

4. Layer the backing, batting and quilt top together and baste. Quilt as desired.
   Note: Since the muslin foundations are not removed, the batting can be eliminated if desired.

5. Sew the binding strips together using diagonal seams to create one continuous strip. Press the strip in half lengthwise, wrong sides together, and sew to the raw edge of the quilt top. Fold binding over raw edges and hand stitch in place.

In the Summertime Coverlet
80" x 96"

UFO Quilt

Finished quilt size approximately: 75" X 96"

Finished block size: 9-1/2"

Quilted by Brenda Brewington

Every quilter has a stash of blocks and fabric pieces left over from previous projects. You may even have an entire quilt top hidden away. It's time to pull that box out of the closet and start cutting those UFOs (UnFinished Objects) into strings for your own unique UFO quilt.

MATERIALS

Note: The orange blocks in the featured quilt are primarily made with UFO blocks that have been cut into strings. The remaining strings were cut from fabrics intended for the original quilt project.

- (48) 10" square foundations for blocks
- (4) 6-1/2" x 55" foundations for side borders
- (4) 6-1/2" x 45" foundations for top/bottom borders
- 5 yards assorted green prints and solids for blocks and borders
- 5 yards assorted orange prints and solids for blocks and borders
- 3/8 yard yellow fabric for accents
- 5/8 yard green fabric for sashing
- 5/8 yard orange fabric for sashing
- 3/4 yard binding fabric
- 6-1/8 yards backing fabric

Note: Fabric requirements may vary depending on the width and placement of strings.

wof = width of fabric

Fabric is 42"-44"-wide unless otherwise noted.

Read through String Piecing Techniques on pages 32-57 before beginning.

CUTTING INSTRUCTIONS

Note: Decide on your string width preference before cutting all the print and solid fabrics into strings.

If using UFO pieces, cut:

A range of 1" - 2-1/2" x wof strings

Cut more 1-1/4" - 1-3/4" strings than other sizes.

Cut some strings across the bias of the blocks and some straight across.

DESIGN ELEMENTS

Unifying elements	• color
	• block shapes
Variation	• fabrics
	• width of strings
	• UFO strings
	• corner sections in varying sizes
Color	• green and orange
	• yellow accents
	• varying values
Line and shape	• blocks oriented to suggest on point squares
	• sashing
	• diagonally pieced borders

From assorted green, orange and yellow fabrics, cut:

1-1/2" selvage strings

A range of 1" - 2-1/2" x wof strings

Cut more 1-1/4" - 1-3/4" strings than other sizes.

Keep strings separate by color.

From orange sashing fabric, cut:

(1) 21" x wof strip. From the strip, cut:

(12) 1-1/4" x 21" strips

(12) 1-1/4" x 19" strips

From green sashing fabric, cut:

(1) 21" x wof strip. From the strip, cut:

(12) 1-1/4" x 21" strips

(12) 1-1/4" x 19" strips

From backing fabric, cut:

(2) 104" x wof pieces

From binding fabric, cut:

(10) 2-1/2" x wof strips

CONSTRUCTING THE BLOCKS

1. Place an assorted green string, right side up, on or near the diagonal center of a 10" foundation square.

2. Lay another green string right side down on the first string, matching the raw edges to be sewn. Secure with pins if desired.

3. Sew the strings together using a ¼" seam. Press the string open.

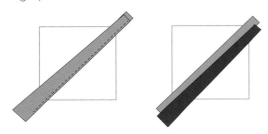

4. Continue sewing green strings on either side of the first string until there is approximately 3-4" of foundation showing in one corner.

5. Sew assorted orange strings to cover the remaining corner. Press to complete a green block. Make 24 green blocks with orange corners.

Note: Sew a variety of string widths and angles within each block. Use an occasional selvage or yellow string as well.

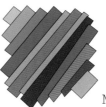

Make 24

6. Repeat to make 24 orange blocks with green corners.

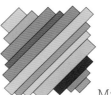

Make 24

PREPARING BLOCKS FOR QUILT TOP ASSEMBLY

1. Press blocks carefully, using starch if needed to stabilize the blocks.

2. Trim blocks to 10" square.

3. Remove the foundation papers.

QUILT TOP CENTER ASSEMBLY

1. Sew the green string blocks together in 6 sets of 4. The orange corners should meet in the center.

Note: When sewing diagonally pieced blocks together, use a ¼" seam allowance. Press seams open.

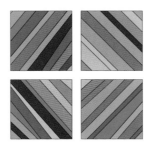 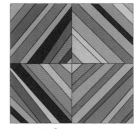

Make 6 sets

2. Sew the orange string blocks together in 6 sets of 4. The green corners should meet in the center.

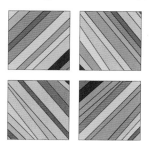
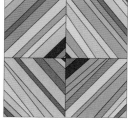

Make 6 sets

3. Sew 1-¼" x 19" orange sashing strips to opposite sides of a green 4-block set. Press the seams toward the sashing.

4. Sew 1-¼" x 21" orange sashing strips to the remaining sides of the green 4-block set. Press the seams toward the sashing. Repeat with the remaining green 4-block sets.

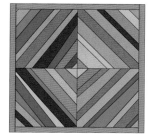

Make 12

5. Repeat with the green sashing strips and the orange 4-block sets.

Make 12

6. Referring to the Quilt Center Assembly Diagram, lay out the 4-block sets in 4 rows with 3 sets in each row.

7. Sew the block sets together in rows. Press seams open. Sew the rows together to complete the quilt center.

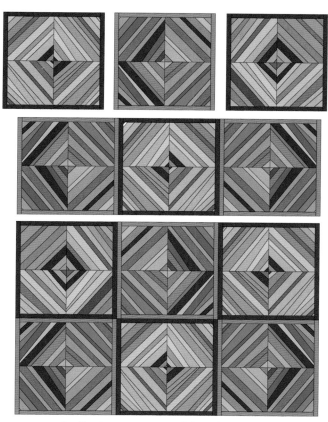

Quilt Center Assembly Diagram

CONSTRUCTING THE BORDERS

Note: Use a variety of strings to make the borders. Each border is made with one left leaning and one right leaning section. The sections are then sewn together.

1. Draw a 45-degree line near the center of (2) 6-½" x 55" foundations. One should be left leaning and one should be right leaning.

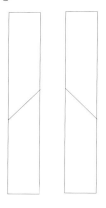

2. Place a string right side up on the foundation, matching a raw edge of the string with the drawn line. Secure with pins if desired. Make sure the string extends past the edges of the foundation.

3. Lay another string right side down on the first string, matching the raw edges to be sewn.

4. Sew the strings together using a ¼" seam. Press the string open.

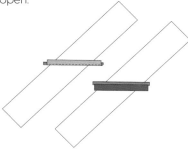

5. Continue adding strings until the foundation is covered. Repeat with the remaining border foundations.

6. Press borders carefully, using starch if needed to stabilize them.

7. Trim borders to size of foundations.

8. Remove the foundation papers.

9. Referring to the photo on page 87 and the diagram, sew the 6-½" x 55" borders together in pairs. Pay attention to the orientation of the strings before sewing.

10. Repeat with the remaining pairs of borders.

Note: The extra border length is for mitering the corners. If you choose not to miter the corners, trim away excess fabric after adding the borders to the quilt center.

ADDING THE BORDERS

1. Matching the center of the quilt top and the center of a 6-½" x 90" top border strip, pin the border strip right side down on the quilt top.

2. Sew the border to the quilt top beginning and ending ¼" from each corner.

3. Repeat steps 1-2 with the bottom and side borders.

4. Lay the quilt top right side up on an ironing board. Extend the borders so the vertical border strip overlays the horizontal one.

5. Fold the vertical border strip at a 45-degree angle and press.

6. Fold the quilt top, right sides together, on the diagonal so the edges of the two border strips align. Pin the borders together along the creased line.

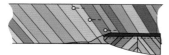

7. Sew on the creased line to make the mitered seam.

8. Trim the seam to ¼" and press open.

9. Repeat on the remaining corners.

FINISHING THE QUILT

1. Sew the 2 backing pieces together as shown. Press seams open.

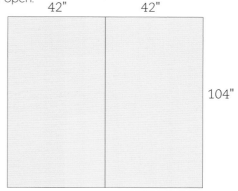

2. Layer the backing, batting and quilt top together and baste. Quilt as desired.

3. Sew the binding strips together using diagonal seams to create one continuous strip. Press the strip in half lengthwise, wrong sides together, and sew to the raw edge of the quilt top. Fold binding over raw edges and hand stitch in place.

UFO Quilt
75" x 96"

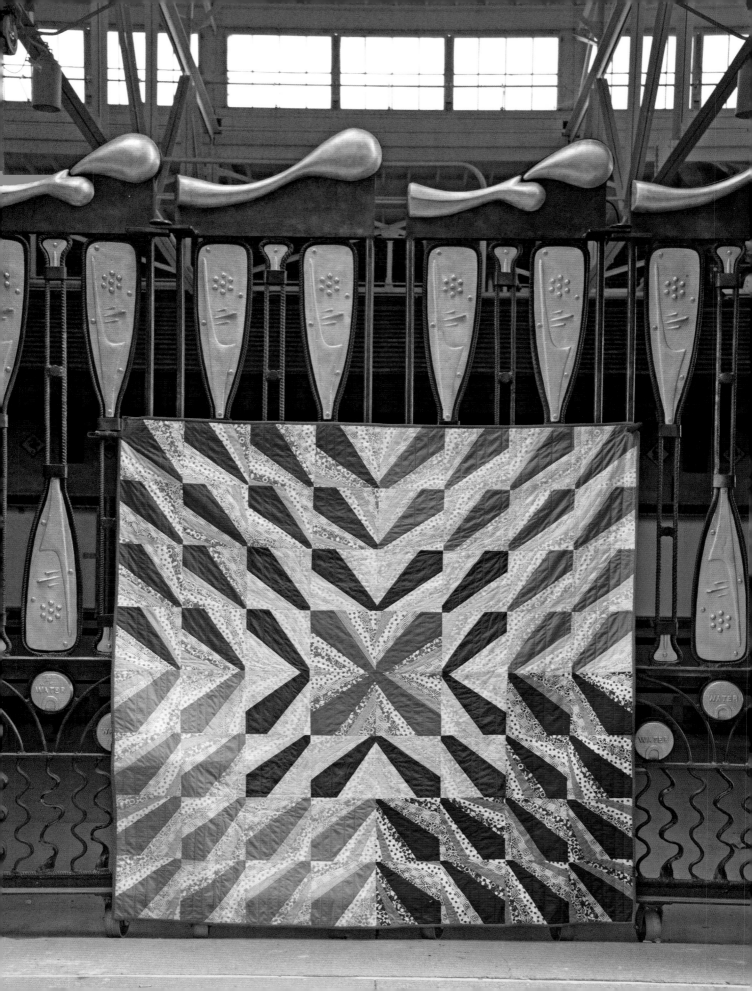

Fan Quilt

Finished quilt size approximately: 72" x 72"
Finished block size: 9"

A group of 30 fat quarters from the same fabric line plus coordinating solids were used to make the Fan quilt blocks. The repetition of the center string moving from the middle out creates a radiating design. The featured quilt uses fat quarters from the Modern Mixers by House for Studio*e* collection.

MATERIALS

- (72) 9-½" square foundations
  (Whisper Web Mesh Light was used in featured quilt)
- (30) assorted print fat quarters divided into 6 color groups with 5 fabrics in each group
- ⅝ yard **each** of 6 coordinating solids for center strings
- ⅝ yard binding fabric
- 4-½ yards backing fabric

Note: Fabric requirements may vary depending on the width and placement of strings.

wof = width of fabric
fat quarter = 18" x 22"
Fabric is 42"-44"-wide unless otherwise noted.
Read through String Piecing Techniques on pages 32-57 before beginning.

CUTTING INSTRUCTIONS

From *each* color group of print fat quarters, cut:

2" x 22" strings for a total of 270 strings

From *each* coordinating solid fabric, cut:

(4) 5" x wof strips. From the strips, cut:
(12) 5" x 14" center strings for a total of 72 center strings
     You will only need 4 red center strings

From backing fabric, cut:

(2) 80" lengthwise pieces

From binding fabric, cut:

(8) 2-½" x wof strips

CONSTRUCTING THE BLOCKS

Note: Each block is made up of a solid center string and coordinating assorted print strings. Refer to Centering One String in a Block on page 40.

1. Draw a diagonal line 2-½" from the center of the foundation square.

DESIGN ELEMENTS

Focal point	• center red fan block
	• solid fan shape in each block
Unifying elements	• sections of same color fans
	• fans going out from center
Variation	• strings surrounding each fan vary
Color	• 6 color groups
Line and shape	• fans radiating out from the center

2. Place a solid center string right side up on the foundation square, matching the right raw edge of the string with the drawn line. Secure with pins if desired. Trim the bottom corners of the string at an angle so the edges of the foundation are easier to see.

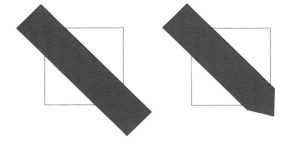

3. Lay a coordinating 2" assorted print string right side down and at an angle on the center string as shown. Position the bottom right of the strip approximately ½" above the bottom right corner of the foundation.

4. Sew the string in place. Fold the foundation paper back and trim any excess fabric. Take care not to cut the foundation.

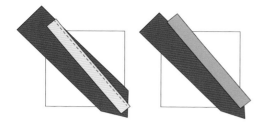

5. Continue adding strings at an angle to either side of the center string.

Note: Beginning at the top of the block, match the raw edge of each new string with the raw edge of the sewn string. Angle the string toward the bottom of the block so it is approximately ½" from the previous seam. Angling the strings in this manner creates the radiating design within each block.

6. Trim any excess fabric after adding each string. Press string open to complete the block. Make a total of 4 blocks in one color way and 12 blocks in each of the remaining color ways.

PREPARING BLOCKS FOR QUILT TOP ASSEMBLY

1. Press blocks carefully. Use starch if needed to stabilize the blocks.

2. Trim blocks to 9-½" square.

3. If not using permanent foundations, remove the foundation papers.

QUILT TOP ASSEMBLY

1. Sew the fan blocks together in 16 sets of 4. Pay attention to the color and orientation of the blocks in each set. Refer to Quilt Top Assembly Diagram for block orientation.

Note: When sewing diagonally pieced blocks together, use a ¼" seam allowance. Press seams open.

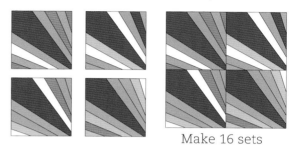

Make 16 sets

2. Referring to the Quilt Top Assembly Diagram, lay out the 4-block sets in 4 rows with 4 sets in each row.

3. Sew the block sets together in rows. Press seams open. Sew the rows together to complete the quilt top.

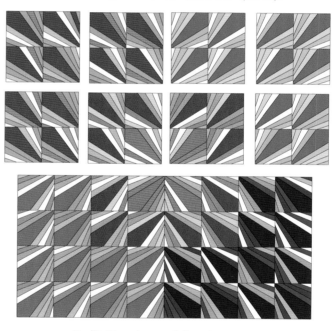

Quilt Top Assembly Diagram

FINISHING THE QUILT

1. Sew the 2 backing pieces together as shown. Press seams open.

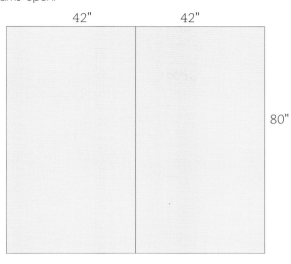

2. Layer the backing, batting and quilt top together and baste. Quilt as desired.

3. Sew the binding strips together using diagonal seams to create one continuous strip. Press the strip in half lengthwise, wrong sides together, and sew to the raw edge of the quilt top. Fold binding over raw edges and hand stitch in place.

Fan Quilt
72" x 72"

Selvage Pinwheels Quilt

Finished quilt size approximately: 52" x 52"
Finished block size: 6"

Selvage strings create stripes when sewn into blocks. The Selvage Pinwheels quilt uses selvages that are at least 1-½"-wide. The blocks go together quickly due to a solid triangle covering one side of each foundation square. When the blocks are sewn together in groups of four they form pinwheels. Regular fabric strings can be used instead of selvages if desired.

MATERIALS

- (64) 6-½" square foundations
- Assorted 1-½" selvage strings for blocks
- 1-⅔ yards teal fabric for blocks and borders
- ½ yard green fabric for blocks
- ½ yard binding fabric
- 2-⅞ yards backing fabric

Note: Fabric requirements may vary depending on the width and placement of strings.

wof = width of fabric
Fabric is 42"-44"-wide unless otherwise noted.
Read through String Piecing Techniques on pages 32-57 before beginning.

DESIGN ELEMENTS

Unifying elements	• blue and green large triangles
	• selvage strips
Focal point	• green triangles in center of quilt
Variation	• many different selvage fabrics
Color	• dark value triangles
	• light value selvages
Line and shape	• pinwheel blocks
	• lines (stripes) produced by selvages

CUTTING INSTRUCTIONS

Note: The half-square triangles are oversized and will be trimmed after blocks are complete. Refer to Making Two Half-Square Triangles on a Single Block on page 50.

From teal fabric, cut:

(5) 7-¼" x wof strips. From the strips, cut:
(24) 7-¼" squares. Cut each square in half diagonally to make a total of 48 half-square triangles.
(8) 2-½" x wof border strips

From green fabric, cut:

(2) 7-¼" x wof strips. From the strips, cut:
(8) 7-¼" squares. Cut each square in half diagonally to make a total of 16 half-square triangles.

From backing fabric, cut:

(1) 60" x wof piece
(2) 21" x wof pieces

From binding fabric, cut:

(6) 2-½" x wof strips

CONSTRUCTING THE BLOCKS

1. Draw a diagonal line ¼" from the center of a foundation square.

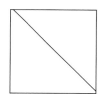

2. Place a teal half-square triangle right side up on a foundation square, matching the right raw edge of the triangle on the drawn line. Secure with pins if desired.

3. Place a selvage string right side up on the triangle, overlapping it approximately ¼". Pin the selvage in place. Sew the selvage in place using a zigzag stitch to cover the edge of the selvage. Press.

Note: If using a straight stitch, stitch right at the finished edge of the selvage.

4. To complete the block, continue adding selvages until the foundation is covered. Make a total of 48 teal blocks.

Make 48

5. Referring to steps 1-4, make a total of 16 green blocks.

Make 16

PREPARING BLOCKS FOR QUILT TOP ASSEMBLY

1. Press blocks carefully, using starch if needed to stabilize the blocks.

2. Trim blocks to 6-½" square.

3. Remove the foundation papers.

QUILT CENTER ASSEMBLY

1. Sew the selvage string blocks together in 16 sets of 4. Pay close attention to the orientation of the blocks. Make (12) teal block sets and (4) green block sets.

Note: When sewing diagonally pieced blocks together, use a ¼" seam allowance. Press seams open.

Make 12 sets   Make 4 sets

2. Referring to the Quilt Center Assembly Diagram, lay out the block sets in 4 rows with 4 block sets in each row.

3. Sew the block sets together in rows. Press seams open.

4. Sew the rows together to complete the quilt center.

Quilt Center Assembly Diagram

ADDING THE BORDERS

1. Sew the 2-½" border strips together end to end in pairs to make 4 border strips.

2. Measure the quilt center from side to side and cut 2 border strips to this size. Sew the strips to the top and bottom of the quilt center. Press seams toward the border.

3. Measure the quilt center from top to bottom and cut 2 border strips to this size. Sew the strips to opposite sides of the quilt center. Press seams toward the border to complete the quilt top.

FINISHING THE QUILT

1. Sew the (2) 21" x wof backing pieces together end to end to make a 21" x 84" piece.

2. Sew the 60" x wof backing piece to the 21" x 84" section as shown. Press seams open.

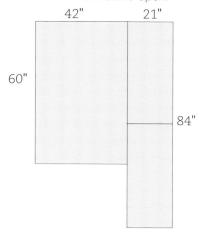

3. Trim away any excess length.

4. Layer the backing, batting and quilt top together and baste. Quilt as desired.

5. Sew the binding strips together using diagonal seams to create one continuous strip. Press the strip in half lengthwise, wrong sides together, and sew to the raw edge of the quilt top. Fold binding over raw edges and hand stitch in place.

Note: An extra block sewn to the back of the quilt makes the perfect label.

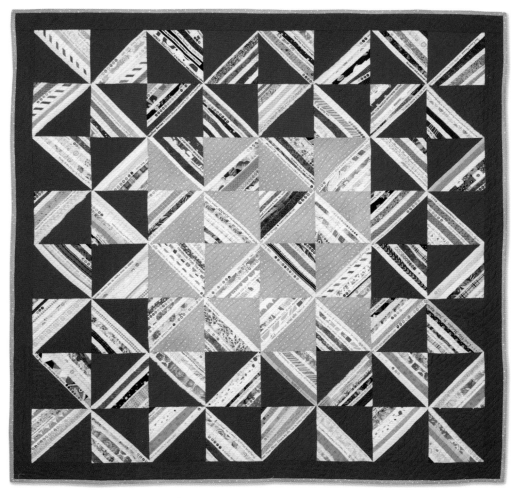

Selvage Pinwheels Quilt
52" x 52"

Simple Modern Squares Quilt

Finished quilt size approximately: 65" x 82-1/2"

Finished block size: 8"

Quilted by Yessant Habetz

The print and white fabric combination gives this quilt a modern look. The string blocks are sewn together in 4-block sets with each set using the same fabric and string width. Consistent string widths and precise placement result in perfect square-in-a-square blocks. Each 4-block set is different from the others. The featured quilt uses a variety of Riley Blake fabrics.

MATERIALS

- (48) 8-1/2" square foundations for blocks
- (58) 4-1/2" square foundations for border
- (8) 4-1/2" x 5" foundations for border
- ¾ yard **each** of 6 assorted print fabrics for blocks and border
- 3-1/2 yards white fabric for blocks, border blocks and cornerstones
- 2 yards blue fabric for sashing, border blocks and outer border
- ⅝ yard binding fabric
- 5-1/4 yards backing fabric

Note: Fabric requirements may vary depending on the width and placement of strings.

wof = width of fabric

Fabric is 42"-44"-wide unless otherwise noted.

Read through String Piecing Techniques on pages 32-57 before beginning.

DESIGN ELEMENTS

Unifying elements	• squares within squares
	• limited number of print fabrics
Variation	• each 4-block set varies order of prints and width of strings
Color	• white, prints and blue
	• blue as darkest value stands out visually
Line and shape	• squares within squares
Proportion	• sashing and border size relative to quilt center
	• the narrower strings in border blocks are in proportion to the smaller size of the blocks

CUTTING INSTRUCTIONS

Note: The 6 assorted print fabrics will be cut in the Constructing the Blocks and Constructing the Borders sections.

From white fabric, cut:

(5) 3-1/2" x wof strips. From the strips, cut:

(48) 3-1/2" squares. Cut each square in half diagonally to make a total of 96 half-square triangles for corners. Triangles are oversized and will be trimmed after blocks are complete.

(1) 2" x wof strip. From the strip, cut:

(20) 2" cornerstone squares

From remaining white fabric, cut:

1-1/2" x wof center strings

From blue fabric, cut:

(16) 2" x wof strips. From the strips, cut:

(31) 2" x 16" sashing strips

(8) 2" x wof outer border strips

Set aside the remaining blue fabric for the border blocks.

From backing fabric, cut:

(2) 92" x wof pieces

From binding fabric, cut:

(9) 2-1/2" x wof strips

Note: The featured quilt uses 3 fabrics for the binding.

CONSTRUCTING THE BLOCKS

Note: Strings of identical width and color or print are used in sets of four blocks. White center strings and half-square triangles are also used in each block. When the sets of blocks are sewn together they create a square-in-a-square. Make each set of four blocks separately.

Determine the color and width of strings desired and cut them as you need them for each set of blocks. Suggested string width is 1-¼" - 2". Vary the width of the strings within the blocks to add interest.
Refer to Centering One String in a Block on page 40.

1. Draw a diagonal line ¾" from the center of an 8-½" foundation square.

2. Place a 1-½" white string right side up on the foundation square, matching the right raw edge of the string with the drawn line. Secure with pins if desired.

3. Select a print fabric and determine the desired width of the string. Cut 4 strings the width chosen. Lay one of the print strings right side down on top of the center string, matching the raw right edges. Secure with pins if desired. Set the remaining three strings aside for the other blocks in the set.

4. Sew the strings together using a ¼" seam allowance. Press the string open.

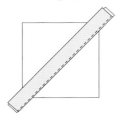 

5. Referring to steps 3-4, sew a different print string to the left side of the center string.

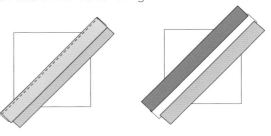

6. Sew a 1-½" white string to either side of the sewn strings. Press the strings open.

7. Referring to steps 3-4, sew print strings to either side of the sewn strings. Press strings open.

8. Sew 3-½" white half-square triangles to opposite corners of the foundation square. Press the triangles open to complete a block. Using the set aside strings, make a total of 4 identical blocks to complete 1 block set.

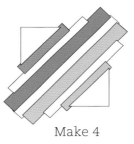

Make 4

9. Make a total of 12 block sets with 4 identical blocks in each set.

PREPARING BLOCKS FOR QUILT TOP ASSEMBLY

1. Press blocks carefully, using starch if needed to stabilize the blocks.

2. Trim blocks to 8-½" square.

3. Remove the foundation papers.

QUILT CENTER ASSEMBLY

1. Sew 4 identical blocks together to make a set. Make 12 identical block sets.

Note: When sewing diagonally pieced blocks together, use a generous ¼" seam allowance. Press seams open.

 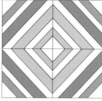

Make 12 sets

2. Referring to the Quilt Center Assembly Diagram, lay out the block sets, blue sashing strips and white cornerstones in rows as shown.

3. Sew the pieces together in rows. Press seams open. Sew the rows together to complete the quilt center.

Quilt Center Assembly Diagram

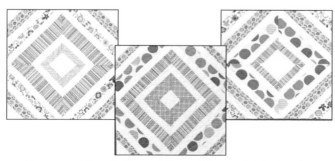

Use a variety of string widths within each block set.

CONSTRUCTING THE BORDERS

Note: The block borders can be trimmed to size, if necessary, after being added to the quilt center. Since the blocks are scrappy, any trimming or adjustments are not noticeable in the finished quilt.

Note: Decide on your string width preference before cutting all the print and solid fabrics into strings.

From remaining assorted print, blue and white fabrics, cut:

A range of ¾" - 2" x wof strings

Note: Cut more 1" - 1-½" strings than other sizes. Since the blocks are small, using narrower strings will look better proportionally.

1. Place a print, blue or white fabric string, right side up, near the diagonal center of a 4-½" foundation square.

2. Lay another string right side down on the first string, matching the raw edges to be sewn. Secure with pins if desired.

3. Sew the strings together using a ¼" seam. Press the string open.

4. Continue sewing strings on either side of the first string.

Note: Sew a variety of string widths and angles within each block.

5. Cover the foundation to complete a block. Make a total of (58) 4-½" blocks.

Make 58

6. In the same manner, make a total of (8) 4-½" x 5" blocks.

Make 8

PREPARING BLOCKS FOR BORDER ASSEMBLY

1. Press blocks carefully, using starch if needed to stabilize the blocks.

2. Trim blocks to 4-½" square and 4-½" x 5".

3. Remove the foundation papers.

ADDING THE BORDERS

1. Referring to the Quilt Assembly Diagram, sew (9) 4-½" square border blocks and (4) 4-½" x 5" border blocks together in a row, alternating the direction of the strings and mixing the block sizes as you sew. Press seams open to complete a top/bottom border. Make 2 top/bottom borders.

2. Sew the top/bottom borders to the top and bottom of the quilt center. Press seams toward borders. Trim the borders even with the quilt center if necessary.

3. Sew (18) 4-½" square border blocks together in a row, alternating the direction of the strings. Press seams open to complete a side border. Make 2 side borders.

4. Sew the side borders to the sides of the quilt center. Press seams toward borders. Trim the borders even with the top and bottom borders if necessary.

5. Sew the 2" blue outer border strips together end to end to make one strip.

6. Measure the quilt center from top to bottom and cut 2 border strips to this size. Sew the strips to opposite sides of the quilt center. Press seams toward the border.

7. Measure the quilt center from side to side and cut 2 border strips to this size. Sew the strips to the top and bottom of the quilt center. Press seams toward the border.

Quilt Assembly Diagram

FINISHING THE QUILT

1. Sew the 2 backing pieces together as shown. Press seams open.

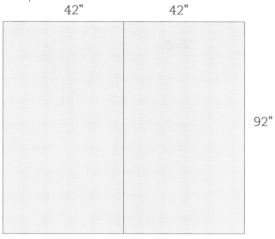

2. Layer the backing, batting and quilt top together and baste. Quilt as desired.

3. Sew the binding strips together using diagonal seams to create one continuous strip. Press the strip in half lengthwise, wrong sides together, and sew to the raw edge of the quilt top. Fold binding over raw edges and hand stitch in place.

Simple Modern Squares Quilt
65" x 82-½"

Juggling Summer Quilt
76" x 92"

Tumbling Triangles Quilt

Finished quilt size approximately: 64" x 64"
Finished block size: 8"

Quilted by Yessant Habetz

Solid floating triangles surrounded by the same color strings in different values make up the blocks in the Tumbling Triangles quilt. The featured quilt uses a single fabric line, Pie Making Day by Brenda Ratliff for RJR Fabrics, plus white and other solids, but feel free to dig into your stash for a super scrappy look.

MATERIALS

Note: The featured quilt is made with 7 colors in a variety of prints and solids.

- (64) 8-½" square foundations
- (4) ⅜ yard assorted print fabrics in **each** of the following color ways: yellow, orange, teal, light blue, green, gray and raspberry for blocks
- (1) ⅜ yard solid fabric in **each** of the following color ways: yellow, orange, teal, light blue, green, gray and raspberry for blocks and center triangles
- ⅛ yard solid white fabric for blocks
- ½ yard binding fabric
- 4 yards backing fabric

Note: Fabric requirements may vary depending on the width and placement of strings.

wof = width of fabric

Fabric is 42"-44"-wide unless otherwise noted.

Read through String Piecing Techniques on pages 32-57 before beginning.

DESIGN ELEMENTS

Unifying elements	• triangles in blocks
	• monochromatic strings surrounding triangles
Variation	• width and angles of strings
	• triangle shape and orientation
	• occasional white or selvage strings
Color	• 7 colors
	• varying values
Line and shape	• triangles
Proportion	• size of triangles to squares

CUTTING INSTRUCTIONS

Note: Decide on your string width preference before cutting all the print and solid fabrics into strings. Separate strings into color groups after cutting.

From *all* assorted print fabrics, cut:

1-½" selvage strips

A range of 1" - 2-½" x wof strings
Cut more 1-¼" - 1-¾" strings than other sizes.

From *each* solid fabric (except white), cut:

(1) 5" x wof strip. From the strip, cut:
64 triangles in a variety of sizes for the block centers. Freehand cut the triangles using a ruler to the keep the sides straight.

From remaining solid fabrics, cut:

A range of 1" - 2" x wof strings
Cut more 1-¼" - 1-¾" strings than 2" strings.

From white solid fabric, cut:

1" x 1-¼" strings

From binding fabric, cut:

(7) 2-½" x wof strips

Note: The featured quilt use 2 solid fabrics for the binding.

From backing fabric, cut:

(2) 72" x wof pieces

CONSTRUCTING THE BLOCKS

Note: Refer to Making Floating Triangles on page 46 when constructing the blocks.

1. Place a solid triangle, right side up, on or near the center of a foundation square.

2. Working with a contrasting color group, lay an assorted print string right side down on the triangle, matching the raw edges to be sewn. Make sure the string extends past the edge of the triangle. Secure with pins if desired.

3. Sew the string in place using a ¼" seam. Sew from triangle edge to triangle edge. Press the string open.

4. Fold the foundation paper back and trim the string even with the triangle edges. Take care not to cut the foundation.

5. Continuing in the same manner and with the same color group, sew strings around the triangle until the foundation is covered.

Note: Sew a variety of string widths and angles within each block. Use an occasional selvage or white string as well.

6. Repeat to make 64 triangle blocks.

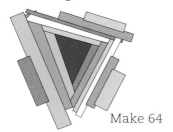

Make 64

PREPARING BLOCKS FOR QUILT TOP ASSEMBLY

1. Press blocks carefully, using starch if needed to stabilize the blocks.

2. Trim blocks to 8-½" square.

3. Remove the foundation papers.

QUILT TOP ASSEMBLY

1. Sew the triangle blocks together in 16 sets of 4.

Note: When sewing string-pieced blocks together, use a ¼" seam allowance. Press seams open.

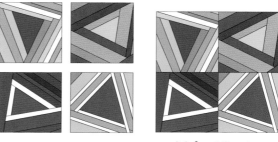

Make 16 sets

2. Referring to the Quilt Top Assembly Diagram, lay out the 4-block sets in 4 rows with 4 sets in each row.

3. Sew the block sets together in rows. Press seams open. Sew the rows together to complete the quilt top.

Quilt Top Assembly Diagram

FINISHING THE QUILT

1. Sew the 2 backing pieces together as shown. Press seams open.

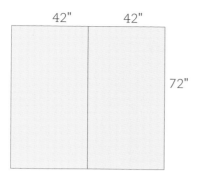

2. Layer the backing, batting and quilt top together and baste. Quilt as desired.

3. Sew the binding strips together using diagonal seams to create one continuous strip. Press the strip in half lengthwise, wrong sides together, and sew to the raw edge of the quilt top. Fold binding over raw edges and hand stitch in place.

Selvages are a fun way to add interest to a block.

Tumbling Triangles Quilt
64" x 64"

Solid Squares Quilt
55" x 66"

String Circles Quilt

Finished quilt size approximately: 72" x 84"
Finished block size: 12"

When I was gifted with a group of batik strips and pieces, I began making string circles. Large round coffee filters made ready-to-use foundations and since batiks don't fray I didn't need a fusible product to appliqué the circles to the black background.

MATERIALS

- (42) large coffee filters
  OR (42) 9-½" circle foundations
- 6-½ yards assorted batik fabrics
  for string circles
- 5-¼ yards black fabric for circle backgrounds
- ¾ yard binding fabric
- 5 yards backing fabric

Note: Fabric requirements may vary depending on the width and placement of strings.
wof = width of fabric
Fabric is 42"-44"-wide unless otherwise noted.
Read through String Piecing Techniques on pages 32-57 before beginning.

DESIGN ELEMENTS

Focal point	• multicolored circles on black background
Unifying elements	• batik fabrics
	• circles
Variation	• assorted colors
	• width of strings
	• circle orientation
Color	• high intensity colors
	• value contrast between background and circles
Line and shape	• circles and lines within circles created by strings
Proportion	• circle size relative to block size

CUTTING INSTRUCTIONS

Note: Decide on your string width preference before cutting assorted batiks fabrics into strings.

From assorted batik fabrics, cut:

A range of 1" - 2-½" x wof strings
Cut more 1-¼" - 1-¾" strings than other sizes.
If using scraps, strings 10" long are sufficient to cover the circle foundations.

From black fabric, cut:

(42) 12-½" squares

From binding fabric, cut:

(9) 2-½" x wof strips

From backing fabric, cut:

(2) 9" x wof pieces

(2) 80" x wof pieces

CONSTRUCTING THE BLOCKS

Note: Press the coffee filter foundations to flatten them.

1. Place an assorted batik string, right side up, on or near the center of a foundation circle. Make sure the string covers the foundation at the top and bottom.

2. Lay another batik string right side down on the first string, matching the raw edges to be sewn. Secure with pins if desired.

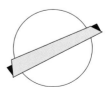

3. Sew the strings together using a ¼" seam. Press the string open.

4. Continue adding assorted batik strings to either side of the center string.

Note: Sew a variety of string widths and angles within each block. Make sure each new string will cover the foundation when opened and pressed.

5. Cover the foundation to complete a string circle. Make a total of 42 string circles.

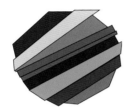

Make 42

PREPARING BLOCKS FOR QUILT TOP ASSEMBLY

1. Press string circles carefully, using starch if needed to stabilize the circles.

2. Using the foundation as the template, trim the excess fabric and ¹⁄₁₆" - ⅛" of the foundation. This will produce a cleaner edge than just cutting away the fabric. Use a good fabric shears instead of a rotary cutter.

3. Fold a 12-½" black square in half lengthwise and finger press. Fold in half widthwise and finger press. Repeat with a string circle. Match the pieces at the folds, both right side up. Pin the string circle in place on the black square to secure it.

4. Using a decorative or zigzag stitch, appliqué the circle to the square.

5. Turn the block to the wrong side and carefully cut away the background square fabric approximately ½" away from the inside edge of the circle to reveal the foundation.

6. Remove the foundation paper and press the block.

Note: A bent tweezers is helpful in removing the foundation near the stitching.

7. Repeat to make a total of 42 blocks.

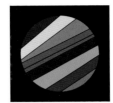

Make 42

> Not using batiks? Use lightweight fusible interfacing to prepare the circles for appliqué.
>
> 1. Place an untrimmed string circle face down on the fusible side of a lightweight fusible interfacing square.
> 2. Sew the string circle in place 1/4" from the edge of the foundation. Trim with scissors along the edge of the foundation.
> 3. Make a slit in the interfacing and turn the circle right side out. Finger press the edges making a smooth circle. Continue with steps 4-6 to complete the block.

QUILT TOP ASSEMBLY

1. Referring to the Quilt Top Assembly Diagram, lay out the blocks in 7 rows with 6 blocks in each row.

2. Sew the blocks together in rows using ¼" seams. Press seams open.

3. Sew the rows together to complete the quilt top.

Quilt Top Assembly Diagram

FINISHING THE QUILT

1. Sew the (2) 9" x wof backing pieces together end to end to make a 9" x 84" piece.

2. Sew the (2) 80" x wof backing pieces to either side of the 9" x 84" piece. Press seams open.

3. Layer the backing, batting and quilt top together and baste. Quilt as desired.

4. Sew the binding strips together using diagonal seams to create one continuous strip. Press the strip in half lengthwise, wrong sides together, and sew to the raw edge of the quilt top. Fold binding over raw edges and hand stitch in place.

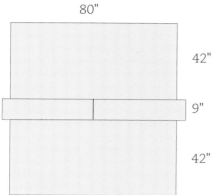

80"

42"

9"

42"

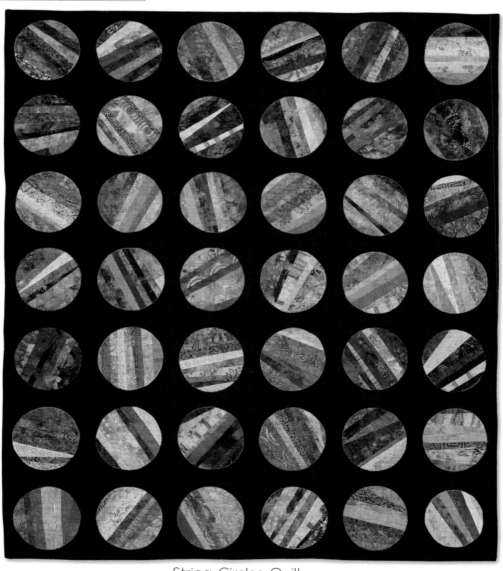

String Circles Quilt
72" x 84"

Leftover Columns Quilt

Finished quilt size approximately: 66" x 61"
Finished column sizes: various widths x 57"

The Leftover Columns quilt is made using leftover strings from the projects in this book. The column size and string orientation changes throughout the quilt. A dark sashing unifies the quilt and its many different fabrics.

MATERIALS

Note: The featured quilt uses strings and selvages left over from other projects.

- (2) 10" x 60" foundations for columns
- (2) 8" x 60" foundations for columns
- (1) 7" x 60 foundation for column
- (2) 6" x 60" foundations for columns
- 5-6 yards assorted fabrics for columns
- 2 yards dark value fabric for sashing, borders and binding
- 4-¼ yards backing fabric

Note: Fabric requirements may vary depending on the width and placement of strings.

wof = width of fabric

Fabric is 42"-44"-wide unless otherwise noted.

Read through String Piecing Techniques on pages 32-57 before beginning.

CUTTING INSTRUCTIONS

Note: Decide on your string width preference before cutting all the fabrics into strings.

From assorted fabrics, cut:

1-½" selvage strips

A range of 1" - 2-½" x wof strings

Cut more 1-¼" - 1-¾" strings than other strings.

From dark value fabric, cut:

(10) 2-½" x 72" strips for sashing and borders

(4) 2-½" x 72" binding strips

From backing fabric, cut:

(2) 76" x wof pieces

DESIGN ELEMENTS

Unifying elements	• sashing and borders
Variation	• column width
	• orientation of strings
Color	• assorted
Line and shape	• diagonal columns
	• straight sashing

CONSTRUCTING THE COLUMNS

Note: Some of the columns have left leaning strings and some have right leaning strings. Refer to the Column Diagram on page 124 and the photo on page 125 as you construct the columns.

1. Draw a 45-degree line near the center of (2) 10" x 60" foundations. One should be left leaning and one should be right leaning.

2. Place a string right side up on a foundation, matching a raw edge of the string with the drawn line. Secure with pins if desired. Make sure the string extends past the edges of the foundation.

3. Lay another string right side down on the first string, matching the raw edges to be sewn. Sew the strings together using a ¼" seam allowance. Press the string open.

4. Continue adding strings to either side of the first string until the foundation is completely covered. Make sure each new string will cover the foundation when opened and pressed.

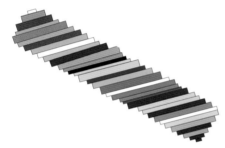

5. Trim the top and bottom of the column even with the foundations.

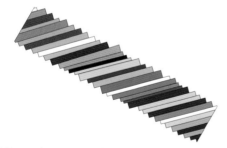

6. Fold the column in half, right sides together, matching the top, bottom and sides of the foundation. Pin and press the fold.

7. Fold the string column in half again, aligning the first fold with the straight edges at the top. Pin. Continue folding the column until it is a manageable size to trim.

8. Using a ruler and rotary cutter, trim the sides of the column to the intended width.

9. Referring to steps 1-8 and the Column Diagram, sew strings to the remaining columns..

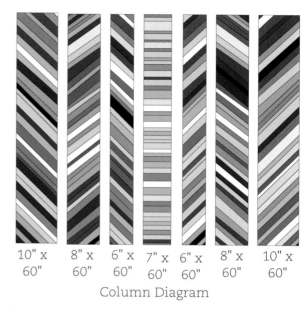

| 10" x 60" | 8" x 60" | 6" x 60" | 7" x 60" | 6" x 60" | 8" x 60" | 10" x 60" |

Column Diagram

10. Unfold the columns and trim each to 57" long. Press columns carefully, using starch if needed to stabilize the columns.

11. Remove the foundation papers.

QUILT CENTER ASSEMBLY

1. Sew (10) 2-½" x 72" dark value strips together end to end to make one strip.

2. Cut (6) 2-½" x 57" sashing strips. The remaining strip will be used for the borders.

3. Referring to the Quilt Center Assembly Diagram, lay out the string columns and sashing strips as shown.

4. Sew the pieces together. Press seams toward the sashing to complete the quilt center. Trim any excess fabric if needed

Quilt Center Assembly Diagram

ADDING THE BORDERS

1. Measure the quilt center from top to bottom and cut 2 border strips to this size. Sew the strips to opposite sides of the quilt center. Press seams toward the border.

2. Measure the quilt center from side to side and cut 2 border strips to this size. Sew the strips to the top and bottom of the quilt center. Press seams toward the border to complete the quilt top.

FINISHING THE QUILT

1. Sew the 2 backing pieces together as shown. Press seams open.

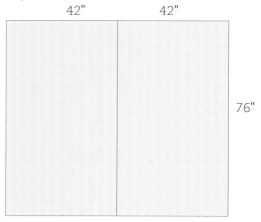

2. Layer the backing, batting and quilt top together and baste. Quilt as desired.

3. Sew the binding strips together using diagonal seams to create one continuous strip. Press the strip in half lengthwise, wrong sides together, and sew to the raw edge of the quilt top. Fold binding over raw edges and hand stitch in place.

Leftover Columns Quilt
66" x 61"

Terms and Definitions

Abstract: using line, color, and shape for a composition that is not representational

Binding: provides a line around the edge of a quilt

Blenders: fabrics that have some texture, but look nearly like solids

Borders: used to frame the quilt design and give it a finished look

Crooked strings: strings that are sewn on other strings at an angle

Diagonal square: created when strings are sewn diagonally to a foundation square

Disappearing strings: strings that don't make it all the way from one end of the block to the other

Fabric line: collection of coordinated fabrics from a specific designer or fabric company; fabric lines change frequently

Fabric style: includes dozens of categories including Civil War reproduction, novelty prints, solids, batiks, 1930's reproduction, geometric and many more

Focal point: center of interest or where viewer's eye is drawn

Geometric: stripes, dots, chevrons, circles, plaid fabrics

Hue: shade or name of the color such as blue, green, gray, purple, etc.

Intensity: the strength or vividness of a color

Line: created by sashing or strings between or within blocks

Monochromatic: having one color or shades of one color

Novelty: representational fabrics ranging from cartoon-like and playful to very realistic

Permanent foundations: foundations that are left in place after strings are sewn to them; generally created with muslin

Proportion: balance of sashing, border and block size in relation to the whole quilt and its other parts

Removable foundations: paper or paper-type products to which strings are sewn; foundation is removed after strings are trimmed

Representational: fabric that is meant to look like or resemble something that exists in the physical world; for example, cars, pigs, trees, leaves, buttons, flowers

Rough-cut foundations: removable or permanent foundations that are oversized; they are cut to size after strings have been added

Sashing: separates blocks or rows of blocks to add a line element

Shape: squares, triangles, circles that make up block designs

Solids: fabrics that are one color

Strings: strips of fabric of varying widths and shapes

Unifying elements: repetition of shapes, colors or fabric styles

Value: lightness or darkness of the color; the lightest color value is white and the darkest is black

Variation: changing lines, shapes and other elements so they are not repetitive in the design

Acknowledgements

Many people, in many ways, large and small, helped make this book a reality. You know who you are and I thank you.

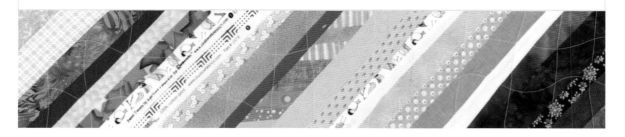